DARK PSYCHOLOGY MASTERY FOR BEGINNERS:

2 BOOKS IN 1:

MANIPULATION & BODY LANGUAGE -
THE COMPLETE GUIDE TO LEARNING
THE ART OF PERSUASION, INFLUENCE
PEOPLE, MIND CONTROL
TECHNIQUES, HYPNOSIS SECRETS AND
NLP MASTERY

Navarro Goleman & Joe Poumpouras

TABLE OF CONTENTS
MANIPULATION AND DARK PSYCHOLOGY

TABLE OF CONTENTS
BODY LANGUAGE AND DARK PSYCHOLOGY

MANIPULATION AND DARK PSYCHOLOGY:

EXPLAINED TECHNIQUES FOR
BEGINNERS: THE COMPLETE GUIDE
TO LEARNING THE ART OF
PERSUASION, INFLUENCE PEOPLE,
MIND CONTROL TECHNIQUES,
HYPNOSIS SECRETS, AND NLP
MASTERY

Navarro Goleman & Joe Poumpouras

Introduction

What Is Manipulation?

Manipulation is a form of social influence that uses indirect, underhanded, and deceptive tactics to change people's perceptions and their resultant behavior. Usually, the end goal is to advance the interests of the person who initiates the manipulation. In many cases, manipulation happens at the expense of the person that is being manipulated; they may be emotionally, mentally, or physically harmed, or they may end up taking actions that are against their own best interests.

It's important to note that social influence is not inherently bad; one person can use manipulation techniques for the good of the person he or she is manipulating. For example, your family members or friends can use social influence and manipulation to get you to do something for your good. The people who mean you well might manipulate you as a way of helping you deal with certain challenges or to help you make the right decisions.

We are more interested in the kind of manipulation that is done with malicious intentions. This is the kind of manipulation that disregards a person's right to accept or reject influence. It is coercive; when the person being targeted tries to push against it, this kind of manipulation gets more sophisticated, and the end goal is to negate the person's will to assert for themselves.

How Manipulation Works

Several psychological theories explain how successful manipulation works. The first and perhaps the most universally accepted theory is one that was put forth by renowned psychologist and author, George Simon. He analyzed the concept of manipulation from the manipulator, and he can up with a pattern of behavior that sums up every manipulation scenario. According to Simon, three main things are involved in psychological manipulation.

First, the manipulator approaches the target by concealing his or her aggressive intentions. Here, the manipulator seeks to endear himself to his target without revealing the fact that his ultimate plan is to manipulate him or her. The manipulator accomplishes this by modifying his behavior and presenting himself as a good-natured and friendly individual, one who relates well with the target.

Secondly, the manipulator will take time to know the victim. The purpose of this is to get to understand the psychological vulnerabilities that the victim may have to figure out which manipulation tactic will be the most effective when he ultimately decides to deploy them.

Depending on the scenario, and the complexity of the manipulation technique, this stage may take anywhere between a few minutes to several years. For example, when a stranger targets you, he may take only a couple of minutes to "size you up" but when your partner or colleague seeks to manipulate you, he or she may spend months or even years trying to understand how your mind works.

The success of this second step depends on how well the first step is executed. If the manipulator successfully hides his intentions from you, he is in a better position to learn your weaknesses because you will instill some level of trust in him, and he will use that trust to get you to let down your guard and to reveal your vulnerabilities to him.   Thirdly, having collected enough information to act upon, the manipulator will deploy a manipulation technique of his choosing. For this to work, the manipulator needs to be able to marshal a sufficient level of ruthlessness; this means that the manipulation technique chosen will depend on what the manipulator can stomach. A manipulator with a conscience may try to use methods that are less harmful to manipulate you. One that completely lacks a conscious may use extreme methods to take advantage of you. Either way, manipulative people are willing to let harm befall their victims, and to them, the resultant outcome (which is usually in their favor) justifies the harm they cause.

Simon's theory of manipulation teaches us the general approach that manipulators use to get what they want from their victims, but it also points out something extremely important: Manipulation works, not just because of the actions of the manipulator, but also because of the reactions of the victims.

In the first step, the manipulator misrepresents himself to the victim: If the victim can see through the veil that the manipulator is wearing, the manipulation won't be successful. In the second step, the manipulator collects information about victims to learn about his or her vulnerabilities. The victim can be may be able to stop the manipulation at this stage by treating the manipulator's prying nature with a bit of suspicion. In the third stage, the manipulator uses coercive or underhanded techniques to get what he wants from the victim. Even in this stage, the victim may have certain choices on how to react to the manipulator's machinations. The point here is that when it comes to manipulation, it takes two to tango. By understanding both the victim's and the manipulator's psychology, it's possible to figure out how you can avoid falling victim to other people's manipulation, and it can also help you become more conscientious so that you don't unknowingly use manipulation techniques on other people around you.

Chapter 1 Theoretical Overview

The work of Dr. Nuccitelli is based upon work completed by Dr. Alfred Adler. At the beginning of the 20th century, Dr. Adler, a medical doctor, psychologist, philosopher, and contemporary of Dr. Carl Jung and Dr. Sigmund Freud, compiled a volume of work exploring many behavioral and psychological theories to explain why some people are prone to commit acts of predatory violence and abuse. From the perspective of Dr. Adler, all human behavior is motivated by a rational purpose. Thus, for Adler, neither good behavior nor bad behavior can be attributed to the basic, fundamental character of the person; instead, all behavior can only be explained by examining the motivations and goals of the person.

For example, a benevolent or kind person behaves in such a manner, not because he or she is a fundamentally kind or caring person, but because he or she has been taught since childhood that kind, caring, and contributory behavior is more likely to result in acceptance by social groups. Further, acceptance into social groups is often an indicator of the likelihood of success in other areas of life.

Similarly, Adler regarded all hostile and predatory behavior as also the result of deliberate purpose and intent. According to Adler, people who commit acts of violence, aggression, or other forms of predation and violation are responding to a deep sense of inferiority. Rejection by a social group can cause the subject of rejection to develop a tendency to move in a negative direction that can lead to further isolation, thereby creating a progressive tendency to develop behavior that is unkind, disrespectful, or otherwise undignified.

Adler, Freud, and Jung all subscribed to the philosophy of teleology, which states that all entities have an end function, goal, or purpose. Under this philosophical construct, all human behavior—good, bad, or otherwise—must be regarded as purposive (i.e., serving some practical purpose). As a result, all human behavior, no matter how deviant, can eventually be understood by examining the practical motives of the actor.

Dr. Nuccitelli has been influential in developing the theories of dark psychology. These theories regard the work of Dr. Adler as extremely important. Dark psychology theory agrees that 99.99% of all human behavior is purposive and can be explained through rational means. However, Nuccitelli differs by insisting that there is .01% of human psychology that is capable of developing harmful and destructive behavior that serves no knowable practical purpose whatsoever. This capacity is what is meant by dark psychology.

Some important terms will help readers understand the language of dark psychology, including Dark Continuum, Dark Factor, Dark Singularity. Because this limits its focus specifically on problems caused by emotional predators and emotional manipulation, we will examine only these three terms.

Dark Continuum: Imagine the Dark Continuum as a line used to gauge the nature and severity of behavior-based in dark psychology. Mild and purposive acts fall to the left of the continuum, while severe and purposeless acts fall to the right.

For example, if we use the Dark Continuum to measure the types of conduct that exhibit traits of dark psychology, then psychological and emotional violations would tend to appear on the left side of the continuum, while acts of physical violence would appear on the right side of the continuum.

Of course, an extremely severe emotional or psychological violation committed for purely sadistic purposes may appear further to the right on the continuum than a less severe act of physical violence committed for a rational purpose.

Dark Factor. The Dark Factor is a term used to describe the latent, inherent capacity of all human beings to act with malevolence. This term expresses a theoretical concept to explain the human propensity to develop personality traits that lead to the likelihood that someone will engage in acts of willful violence, destruction, or harm to others.

Many influences may exacerbate or lessen the chance that the latent capacity for abuse will be activated. However, all people possess a Dark Factor in their psychological makeup.

Dark Singularity. This term is also used to describe a theoretical concept. It borrows from the language of physics, which describes a singularity as the absolute center of a black hole. The singularity at the center of a black hole contains energy and gravity that is so dense and powerful that, as objects approach it, they became ensnared in its gravitational pull to the point that they cannot escape. Even light can become trapped in the singularity of a black hole.

To gain a better understanding of dark psychology, Dr. Nuccitelli has compiled the following six tenets that define the nature and function of dark psychology:

All people possess the capacity for dark psychology. Dark psychology is not a genetic defect or flaw, but a universal aspect of the human condition.

Dark psychology studies the innate human potential for developing predatory behavior that does not serve any practical purpose. Thus, if 99.99% of human behavior is designed to achieve a practical goal, dark psychology represents that .01% capacity within human psychology to engage in conduct with an end-goal of causing pain, harm, and damage.

Dark psychology seeks to fill gaps in the explanation of destructive and harmful human behavior and takes the position that dark psychological behavior traits can manifest themselves anywhere on a continuum of predatory behavior, from mild deviance to extreme violence.

The Dark Continuum is not defined exclusively by the end act of deviance or violence, but by the practical, psychological motivations of the person. For example, Jeffrey Dahmer and Ted Bundy were both serial killers. Yet, Dahmer was motivated by the need for companionship and love, however distorted and delusional; while Bundy was motivated by nothing more than a sadistic desire to inflict pain. Thus, Bundy is further along the continuum of dark psychology than Dahmer, even though both were serial killers.

Dark psychology assumes that all people have the innate capacity for violence. While animals share this capacity, they employ violence to serve the needs of the predator-prey relationship in the natural order. Because human beings have evolved beyond that state, yet still retain the innate capacity for violence, this capacity is distorted in human psychology and may be used to act in violence without a practical purpose.

Following are four profiles of criminal personality that have been identified by law enforcement officials and clinical psychologists as exhibiting behavior that exists on the far-right end of the dark continuum:

Arsonists: Arsonists are obsessed with setting fires and commonly have experienced a history of sexual and/or physical abuse. Their dark psychological personality traits are evident in their tendency to live apart from social groups. This isolation tends to further accelerate their decline into self-obsession, which enables them to more easily support their fascination with setting fires. They generally experience a sense of pleasure and happiness when they see their target structures burn.

Necrophiliacs: These are people who exhibit a sexual attraction to corpses. Because necrophiliacs have a difficult time establishing emotional or social bonds with others, their psychological and emotional development is disrupted, and as they move along the Dark Continuum, their attraction to the inanimateness of corpses intensifies.

Serial killers: The FBI defines a serial killer as anyone who commits "a series of three or more killings, not less than one of which was committed within the United States, having common characteristics such as to suggest the reasonable possibility that the crimes were committed by the same actor or actors" (Nuccitelli, 2006).

Clinical psychologists have found that serial killers are motivated by the psychological gratification that can only be achieved through brutality and killing gives them a feeling of released tension and increased power.

iPredators. This group of predators represents a new development in the field of dark psychology because ICT has been in use for only a relatively short amount of time.

Chapter 2 Historical Overview

The foundations of the study of dark psychology are not modern. The models of classical comedy and tragedy during the height of the Greek Empire illustrate an understanding of this uniquely human capacity even during ancient times. The comedies and tragedies of ancient Greek theater were used as a means for society to experience catharsis—a collective exercise in which social bonding occurred by the creation and release of social tensions as a means of resolving societal conflicts.

But what is at the heart of this classical method of employing art as a means of regulating society is society's need to be regulated because of the unique capacity of human beings to act in ways that are destructive and harmful without any apparent practical purpose or necessity. This capacity is what clinical psychologists refer to as dark psychology.

Consider that species other than humans, such as lions, wolves, bears, or birds of prey, may track, target, hunt, and kill smaller, less powerful animals, such as deer, cattle, sheep, rabbits, and rodents. Yet, the reason for this predatory behavior is a necessity, not cruelty or malevolence. Also, when predatory animals hunt, they are likely to target the most vulnerable and the weakest, not out of any sense of meanness or malice, but because engaging with a weaker opponent involves less risk and less effort. Thus, the violence and destruction of natural predators serve practical needs—to feed themselves and their young to propagate their species.

Especially in the modern world, human beings have the advantage of education, positions of professional employment, the ability to grow and cultivate food, advanced language and communication systems, and a complex and interconnected system of world government, law, finance, and banking. As a result, there is no practical reason for any human being to engage in any act of predation or violence to secure the goals of food, shelter, and propagation. Because the system of laws punishes violence, such actions are detrimental to achieving these goals.

These habits and systems of living are unique to the human species, so it is reasonable to assume that they may require responses and abilities among the human members of society that are also unique. For example, lions and wolves are not incapable of becoming doctors, plumbers, mechanics, or politicians, nor will they ever have any interest in doing so. These occupations are unique to the human species.

It is tempting to argue that human beings have developed their unique capacity for dark psychology as a means of propagating their survival in this unique environment. Take for instance a businessman who cheats on his taxes to gain an advantage in the business world, a lawyer who alters evidence to win a case, or a politician who lies to his constituents to win an election may be compared to the abilities of wild bears who hunt and killdeer or other game. Yet, animals in the wild never engage in predatory conduct that is marked by cruelty, maliciousness, or greed. Doing so would lead to their extinction.

We may understand that a business owner or banking professional would use every tool at his or her disposal to gain a competitive advantage. We may even understand the tendency among some professionals to work around laws rather than follow them when they see an economic advantage in doing so—when no real harm results, there is a practical goal that justifies the apparent abuse.

But often, criminal activity in human society does not have any practical justification. Within the unique sphere of human experience, dark psychology itself is a unique phenomenon. Defined broadly, it is the capacity for destructive and harmful behavior that serves no practical purpose whatsoever.

While all human beings have the capacity for dark psychology, many people do not act on these dark urges, choosing instead to channel that energy toward more productive and useful activities. Some people, however, do act on these dark urges to inflict gratuitous pain and harm on others.

Among those who are governed by dark psychology rather than by rational psychology, there is a continuum of deviant behavior ranging from mild forms of manipulation and dishonesty, usually motivated by some type of personal or financial gain; to acts of physical violence; and at the most end of the spectrum, the movement toward the "Dark Singularity," in which a person's psychology becomes so compromised by and addicted to deviant, aberrant, criminal, and malevolent misconduct that it becomes impossible for them ever to return to a rational mental state.

Historical tales of serial killers like Jack the Ripper remind us that this human failure is not new. Unfortunately, modern society appears to have embraced, at least to some limited degree, a complete rejection of all morality and social norms. The anonymity and access to power and information made possible by the invention of the internet has given these elements resources to establish for themselves a viable, permanent presence in human society. Understanding the nature and function of dark psychology has become an indispensable tool for anyone working to achieve success.

Before considering any further what "dark psychology" means, it may be more helpful to consider what "normal" means. Many historians and literary theorists have made the case that the evolution of human civilization has been accompanied by a steady erosion of social, moral, and cultural norms.

The word "more" (with the "e" pronounced as a long a, i.e., MOR-ay) is used to describe the social rules society enforces to encourage acceptable behavior. Many college graduates may remember taking a course from a sociology professor who required as a homework assignment that they deliberately identify and violate a more, then write a paper about the consequences. At one time, it was not uncommon for visitors to a college campus to enter an elevator and find themselves joined by a well-adjusted and successful college student who, for no apparent reason, faced the back of the elevator rather than the doors, thereby forcing uncomfortable and prolonged eye contact. This example of social deviance is very mild and can be viewed as even less threatening when we consider that it occurred in the context of a supervised experiment in the controlled and benign environment of a postsecondary educational institute.

Literature and humanities professors may help students examine this phenomenon in greater, and often more graphic and unforgettable, detail. For example, a pre-internet era literature course at a state university in California examined the transformation of cultural norms from 17th century France up through late 20th century America. In this course, the French novel, La

Princesse de Clèves, was used to set a ground floor of social norms.

This novel portrays the life of a young woman living in the court of Henry II. Her mother had raised her with the greatest discipline to rise to the height of French society. As she enters adulthood, she is escorted to court to secure a prospect for marriage among the young noblemen. She eventually marries a young prince.

Already at this point in the novel, by today's standards, the main character of the novel would be considered successful beyond the reach of most people. However, her life does not proceed according to the ease and happiness we might expect. Instead, royal intrigue, gossip, and power struggles complicate matters. Although no actual wrongdoing ever really takes place, the young princess's hopes and ambitions are ultimately destroyed by the mere suspicion of infidelity. She is ultimately motivated by her sense of duty and obligation to enter a convent, where she dies in obscurity.

The course then uses literary works from intervening eras to trace the decline in the standards of human civilization from the virtuous heights depicted in La Princesse de Clèves through the dawn of the Industrial Revolution and ultimately to modern society at the end of 20th century America. The endpoint is illustrated by the violence, decadence, chaos, and alienation depicted in the late 20th century American novel, Looking for Mr. Goodbar.

In this novel, a young schoolteacher, who, like the princess in the earlier novel, is an accomplished woman occupying an enviable position, is also seeking a prospect. However, her environment—the singles bars of New York City—is far removed from the royal court of 17th century France. Like the princess in the earlier novel, she too suffers a tragic fate at a young age when she is murdered by a young man she has met on one of her social outings.

Thus, defining social norms has become increasingly challenging, and many people have made the case that those norms are eroding as humanity progresses through its evolutionary cycles. We may refer to this tendency to develop destructive, negative, or harmful behavior as "dark psychology."

The emergence of iPredators as a class of offenders identified by clinical psychologists underscores the importance of understanding this area of psychology. New technology has expanded the power and speed through which dark psychology has found a way to manifest itself among many segments of human society; ICT has also magnified the degree to which such lifestyles have made themselves potentially viable, long-term means of living.

The following chart illustrates the differences in the psychological makeup between well-adjusted people with healthy psychology and those who exhibit predominantly dark psychological traits:

Chapter 3 Dark Triad Personalities

S ome claim that the symptoms of the dark personality triad are much like the Bermuda triangle: a pit, a special and dangerous aspect. The explanation for this is very simple: only instrumental objectives are driven by this type of profile. That is, you do not hesitate to compromise others 'rights to achieve your own goals.

As Donald Trump came to power in January 2017, several mental health experts cautioned that a dark triad test could be done under the new US President. We will never know as no evidence is available or any study has been used to validate such a hypothesis.

But those who see features that point in this direction are not missing. The use or abuse of means to achieve personal gain, narcissism, contempt for the thoughts and opinions of others may be more than mere coincidences.

Within the same year of his arrival to influence, there is also an important research published in a journal of Personality Psychology in which this theory is explored and data are provided.

There is, however, an obvious fact. We look at famous figures occasionally. Nevertheless, in some people in our setting, this clinical entity which essentially sums up the human being's most malicious characteristics may present. Also, it is often recognized in the field of psychology that this type of profile is normal in the organization.

The Signs of the Dark Triad of Personality

The dark triad is a concept that came into being in the 1990s. Now, the research and definitions by the University of British Columbia psychologists Paulhus and Williams coined the element in 2002. Now, a significant thing should be noted.

When we talk about the dark triad, we do not speak of a personality disorder; it is a collection of subclinical characteristics that describe an adverse behavior of a sort, and that causes great environmental discomfort.

A person with a high scoring in the dark triad test will have a psychosocial effect in every scene he is going. And these antisocial strategies used by these men and women impact both personal, emotional, and work-related relationships. Let us now study the dark triad signals.

Narcissism

Narcissism is one of the most obvious characteristics of the dark triad. The main core of this trait is selfishness and that constant need for visibility, power, and admiration.

In addition, they usually show the ability to captivate people. They show great power of seduction, they are friendly, they shine at parties, in meetings and they always manage to attract attention due to their outgoing character. However, that charm has a catch; it is an instrumental purpose to move up your ranks, to have alliances, to achieve your goals.

On the other hand, it is important to remember what your Achilles heel is: low self-esteem.

Excess of appreciation and the cult of oneself is called "narcissism", which in the face of psychoanalysis is a fundamental trait in the formation of the human being, being necessary for the constitution of self-love, for confirmation and support of self-esteem. However, like everything, exaggeration can be a sign of some failure. You need to be aware of the signs so that it is not a red light in your personal or professional life.

Popularly, one has the impression that the cult of the ego is something exclusively linked to people of high society or who occupy great positions, showing their achievements and possessions in a snobbish way. However, no group is exempt from the presence of these people. Narcissism is more present in our lives than we can imagine and is most likely to blame for the feeling of unhappiness: it is in the nature of the narcissist to ridicule or belittle so that he can always be in a better position, or to be better regarded.

It is also common to see him seek charity or predictability so that he can anticipate and "win the game". Narcissistic people have chronic dissatisfaction as nothing reaches their ideal expectation, that is, nothing is ever enough.

signs of a narcissistic person?

Since birth, everyone has some level of narcissism, however, the pathology exists only after a certain level, being still in this healthy stage. This is where the question arises: what is the limit between the healthy and the pathological? To answer this question see the topics below:

1 - The leadership

Narcissists need to exercise dominance to feed their egos. However, as the "command" others, since they have the facility to do so, they neglect the needs of their subordinates. The junctions of these items make them bad bosses, although I think the opposite is true. Narcissists are not good leaders and they confuse leadership with authoritarianism.

2 - Center of attention

Narcissistic people are sociable and communicative and establish their relationships in a way that draws a lot of attention from the people around them, they like to have the spotlight on them. Not everyone always sees these people in a good way, as they are always in evidence.

3 - Eccentricity

Narcissists give excessive attention to the stereotype. In this context, they worry excessively about clothes and accessories, often being ostentatious. They are interpreted by those who see them as different and daring people.

4 - Vanity

An excessive cult of the body exists on the part of these people. This point is valued for being natural seducers and they always tend to be directed towards that. It is common to see narcissists exaggerate when doing physical activities in search of perfection, which, many times, they never achieve, because they always want more.

5 - Loving relationships

Narcissists treat their partners as great achievements, displaying them as trophies so that the world can see how they are loved and loved. This need to appear is also constantly expressed within their own relationships, where they have a constant need to always demonstrate to partners the existing interest of others in themselves, and who can betray them at any time.

6 - Self-Improvement

Often, in the search for self-worth, they hurt and distort the image of those around them in an attempt to make their own image, in comparison, better. When they are surrounded by more important people, they tend to devalue them, tarnishing their images, so that in a way, even illusory, they are better in front of others.

Machiavellianism

Machiavellianism differs in one aspect from narcissism: they do not make use of appearances; they do not captivate or seduce. Hence, they tend to impress with their instrumental coldness and, above all, with their manipulative efficiency. In this sense, it is common that one of the signs of the dark triad is the lack of empathy and that insatiable search to achieve what they want.

The person with dark triad traits can be friendly and engaging at first, thus fulfilling the perfect profile of a narcissist. However, if those kindest of gifts do not work, a true Machiavelli will emerge, where the emotional coldness to achieve his goal becomes apparent.

Signs of Machiavellianism

Some of the features of Machiavellianism are characterized by the following trends:

Orientation and concern only with their own ambitions and interests.

Prioritizing money and power in relationships

Striving for the charm and confident appearance

Exploiting and manipulating others for progress

Lying and cheating when needed

Frequent use of flattery

Lack of principles and values

Isolating others when it comes to truly getting to know one's personality

Cynicism about moral standing

Ability to cause others to harm in order to achieve their personal goals

Low levels of empathy

Frequent avoidance of commitment and emotional attachment

Ability to have great patience when it comes to benefits

Rare disclosure of true intentions

The tendency to have casual sexual contacts

Ability to recognize social situations

Lack of warmth in social interactions

Lack of desire for clarity with the consequences of personal actions

Sometimes there is a fear of identifying personal emotions.

Psychopathy

The psychopathic personality is that third echelon that shapes the signs of the dark triad. Now, remember that this dimension does not refer to a psychological disorder. We speak only of one type of personality, with which, the psychopathic traits are usually evidenced as follows:

Emotional insensitivity.

Antisocial behavior (they do not hesitate to skip legal, ethical, and even moral codes).

Impulsiveness.

Predisposition to boredom, constantly need new reinforcements and stimuli.

Lack of regrets and ethical-moral sense.

Lack of commitment to social and affective relationships; many even show sexual promiscuity.

Characteristics of A Psychopath

There are some more common traits that we observe in the behavior and habits of those who have the disorder.

1) Lack of empathy: it is common to think that psychopaths do not have any feeling of empathy for

other people, but in fact, they are able to elect people and moments to show some kind of affection in that sense. This selective choice makes them even more manipulative and disguised in their relationships.

2) Impulsivity: they hardly accept being contradicted, rejected or frustrated, so they react impulsively in a more aggressive and explosive way, without caring about the feeling of involvement of others around.

3) Egocentric and Megalomaniacs: they have exaggerated pride and always think they are right. This certainty of their actions makes them never feel afraid of their actions, they refuse to recognize their actions and, consequently, they are not capable of feeling remorse.

4) Liar: your lie is pathological to the point that they don't even know more when they are inventing something. There is also no concern about not taking advantage of other people's good faith based on the deception that your speech causes.

5) Search for adventures: his inability to feel fear or worry about generating fear in other people, makes the psychopath always look for challenges that test his ability to break rules and escape the monotony behind adrenaline.

6) Anti-social: social rules and parameters do not enter the world of psychopaths, who constantly seek to break

these factors in order to feel grander and prouder of themselves;

7) Lack of emotion: psychopaths do not usually relate to other people for real emotional issues, such as love and affection, but to take advantage of what these people can offer you.

Explore your dark side to regain control over yourself

What feeds your dark side?

The dark side of the mind harbors pain and self-destruction, everything you deny, and the urges you have struggled to satisfy.

Your unfulfilled individual needs to generate negative emotions that will drive them. If these needs are not met, these negative feelings will develop in you, and that will lead to the worst in you.

And you'll think this is the real version of yourself or maybe the only one.

Never feeding the dark part of your mind is the only way of managing it.

And there are other things you shouldn't do because you know because they're detrimental to you, so you're doing them anyway.

You know you shouldn't drink, you shouldn't eat fats, you shouldn't argue with your spouse or kids, you shouldn't feed needless arguments, but you do so anyway.

Your dark side is not healthy, either. Either you act and stop feeding him or he's going to take care of you.

Chapter 4 Differences between Persuasion and Emotional Manipulation

Manipulation is a way to control others, and it can be used in different ways. Some of these ways can be very subtle, and others can be easily recognizable, especially if you know what you are looking for.

With manipulation, one of the first things that a person will notice is the feeling of fear, obligation and/or guilt. When someone is trying to manipulate you, they are trying to coerce you to do something that you don't want to do. You feel scared thinking about doing what they want or feeling scared in the act, there is a feeling of obligation that goes along with it, and you sometimes feel guilty if you don't do it at all.

On the other hand, if they play the victim, they try to make you think that they are hurt. No matter the case, they are often the ones who caused the problem in the first place. If you are being targeted by a manipulator who is playing the victim, you will do whatever they want to stop their suffering. You might even feel responsible for their suffering, even though you are not.

Another thing a person who is being manipulated does is question themselves and what they are doing. This can often be referred to as gaslighting. This type of manipulation has people not only questioning themselves but what is real to them, what they perceive, their own thoughts, and even their memory. Has someone ever twisted your words around and made it about them? Have they taken over the conversation to make you feel like you're the perpetrator and that you did something wrong while you wonder what it is that you exactly did? Gas lighters know how to make their victims feel a false sense of guilt, responsibility and even defensiveness. They will have you questioning if you have done something wrong when you haven't at all.

Another manipulation tactic comes with strings attached. People should want to do things for you just because they want to and not what they can get out of it. This is one of the most common forms of manipulation. You feel like someone is being nice to you and doing things for you when you need them. But there always seems to be a catch or something involved. If you don't adhere to those stipulations, then they make you feel ungrateful, like you are taking advantage of their kindness.

There are other forms of manipulation, but these are the most common forms. It is imperative to know what manipulation is and the different forms so that you can protect yourself against it.

Persuasion can be found in images, sounds and even using words. There is a deliberate attempt to influence others. One of the key points about persuasion is that people are not coerced or manipulated; instead, they are free to choose what they believe. Even though the images, sounds or words used in advertisements help them choose what others tell them too. Persuasion can be found in advertisements or messages on radio, the internet, television, billboards, and face to face communication through verbal and non-verbal ways.

This technique has increased over the years and especially in the 21st century. Messages in the form of advertisements over different sorts of media have grown and are spread rather rapidly. On average, every U.S. adult is exposed to 300 to 3,000 advertisements every day (Cherry, 2018).

It can even be found within business itself, and we are not talking about advertising agencies. There are a lot of companies that use the art of persuasion to sell goods and services.

Many of the advertisements that we see have been specially made or crafted to get people to buy their products or services because they want to look like them or live that certain lifestyle.

If both manipulation and persuasion are prevalent in advertising, then what are their core differences?

How can you tell them apart?

"Advertising manipulates when it encourages the audience to form untrue beliefs" (Noggle, 2018). This occurs when we are told that fried chicken is healthy, or when the associations that are used are often faulty, like Marlboro cigarettes and the association with the ruggedness of the Marlboro Man. If the manipulation of the Marlboro man is successful, the ads themselves contribute to disease and death. People often think of manipulation as wrong because it harms the person being manipulated. And, this is the case most of the time. But there are times when manipulation itself is not harmful.

Immanuel Kant stated that "morality requires us to treat each other as rational beings rather than mere objects" (Noggle, 2018). The only rational way that we can even try to manipulate people, or their behavior is through rational persuasion, and any other way is just immoral and even unethical.

What makes manipulation wrong?

In any situation, the manipulator tries to get the other person to believe what the manipulator feels is wrong. The manipulator is lying to the other person, and to make the other person make some form of mistake. Thus, they can also make you believe a false statement, make you feel inappropriate, get someone else's approval in the wrong way or to doubt something, even yourself. There is no good reason to get someone to doubt. So, to answer the question above, the core distinction between manipulation and non-manipulation depends on the manipulator and if they are trying to get someone to make some sort of mistake regarding how they feel, think, doubt, or pay attention to something.

Reasonable persuasion, defined by Immanuel Kant, is the only moral way to influence people. It is just considered to be one of the ways that we interact with everyone around us. You might want to persuade someone to think a certain way because you want to see the world become a better place. This is often true when you are debating with someone about their political view of the world and you come back with an intelligent, researched argument that changes their perception. Did you harm them in any way? No, you reasonably persuaded them to come to your side. They made the choice all on their own.

Another way that you can persuade someone is through making a profit. All types of persuasion further some sort of self-interest. There is nothing wrong with making money. It isn't evil, unethical or immoral. However, you have to persuade another person to part with their money by getting them to believe that what you have to sell – whether it is a good or service – is what they want or need.

Jonathan Fields states that the difference between persuasion and manipulation can be defined in three ways:

The intent behind the reason you want to persuade someone

The truth behind the process

The benefit of impact on the person you are trying to persuade

For example, Amber married Devon 2 years ago, and they started to have marital problems during the beginning of their second year of marriage. One-night Devon comes home drunk and hits Amber in the face. The abuse continues from there until one night she wakes up in the hospital with broken bones. Amber's parents are sitting beside the bed, and her mother takes her hand in hers. That night her parents urge her to leave Devon because it is in her best interest. They know she loves him, but he needs to get help for his anger. They persuade her to file domestic violence charges against him because the next time she might not be so lucky, and they can't lose their baby girl.

Now Amber has a choice in all of this. She has the choice to stay with Devon and risk that things will get better or worse. Or she has the choice to leave him with or without pressing charges. Her parent's argument was reasonably persuasive, but they were still giving her a choice. They did not force her or influence her to make a choice. There were quite a few ways, as was stated before, to manipulate the situation and make her do what they wanted, even if that wasn't what she wanted, which would be manipulation. There is no good type of manipulation, only good persuasion.

Amber isn't dumb and knows what she is risking if she goes back to Devon. And, this is where the persuasion influences her to make a choice. The argument her parents brought to her is with love and compassion. They care about her well-being, and they want her to know that she can come home, and everything will be okay. Amber feels good making this decision and is not making it out of remorse, guilt or out of obligation to her family. This is the main and very important difference between persuasion and manipulation.

This is why it is important to know the difference. When you are persuading someone, they often are feeling better for meeting you. Those who are being manipulated, feel guilt the second you leave. (Roberts, 2019).

Chapter 5 What is Emotional Manipulation?

Y ou've likely experienced individuals who are emotionally manipulative and controlling.

They utilize these practices to get their direction or prevent you from saying or doing anything they don't care for.

Emotional manipulation can be unpretentious and misleading, leaving you befuddled and wobbly.

Or then again, it tends to be clear and requesting where fears, disgracing, and remorseful fits leave you shocked and immobilized.

In any case, emotional manipulation isn't worthy, and the more you enable it to proceed, the more force and certainty the manipulator gains in this uneven relationship.

Inevitably, any leftover of a sound association is pulverized, as the establishment of trust, closeness, regard, and security disintegrates under the sled of manipulation.

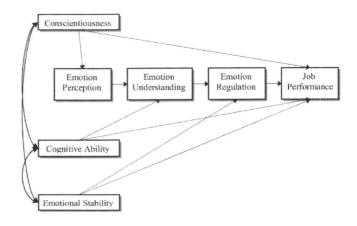

Specific Types of Emotional Manipulation

Within these major categories of emotional manipulation techniques, psychologists have also identified a wide range of more subtle variations that we all likely encounter on a daily basis.

These techniques include:

• Lying: Dark Triad personalities, particularly psychopaths, are highly skilled at lying and cheating, so often we may not detect their intent until it is too late. Beware of those who have demonstrated a pattern of dishonesty.

• Lying by omission: Lying by omission is a little more subtle. The predator may not say anything that is untrue but may withhold information that is necessary in an effort to cause you to fail.

• Denial: Often the damage from emotional manipulation is inflicted after the fact. When you confront someone with evidence of their dishonesty and abuse, their refusal to admit wrongdoing can cause even greater psychological harm.

• Rationalization: The increase in popular news media has led to the growth of public relations and marketing firms who produce "spin" to deflect criticism in both political and corporate environments. Rationalization is a form of spin, in which a manipulator explains away his or her abuse.

• Minimization: Like rationalization, minimization is a form of denial in which the predator understates the seriousness of his or her offense.

• Selective attention and/or inattention: Manipulators will pick and choose which parts of an argument or debate should be considered so that only their views are represented.

• Diversion: Manipulators often resist giving straight answers to questions, particularly when they are confronted by their victim. Instead, they will divert the conversation to some other topic or change the subject altogether.

• Evasion: More serious than diversion, a manipulative person confronted with his or her own guilt will often completely evade responsibility by using long rambling responses filled with so-called "weasel words," like "most people would say," "according to my sources," or other phrases that falsely legitimize their excuses.

• Covert intimidation: Many manipulative people will make implied threats to discourage further inquiries or resolution.

• Guilt tripping: A true form of emotional manipulation, a manipulator will exploit the integrity and conscientiousness of the victim by accusing them of being too selfish, too irresponsible, or not caring enough.

• Shaming: Although shaming can be used to bring about social change when large corporations or governments advance abusive or discriminatory policies, manipulators may attempt to intimidate their victims by using sharp criticism, sarcastic comments, or insults to make them feel bad.

• Blaming the victim: This tactic has become increasingly common. When a victim accuses a predator of abuse, the predator will attempt to turn it around by creating a scenario in which the victim alone is responsible for the harm that came to him.

• Playing the victim: Using the opposite tactic of blaming the victim, the predator will lure a conscientious person into a trap by pretending to have been grievously wounded and cultivating feelings of sympathy. The real plan, however, is to take advantage of the caring nature of the conscientious person by toying with their emotions.

• Playing the servant: This tactic is common in environments marked by a strict, well-established chain of command, like the military. Predators become skilled at manipulating this system by creating a persona of suffering and nobility, in which their bad actions are justified as duty, obedience, and honor.

• Seduction: This technique does not always have to involve sexual conquest or intimacy. Emotional predators may use flattery and charm to convince people to do their bidding, and they often look for people with low self-esteem.

• Projection: This term is used in psychotherapy. Predators who use this technique will look for victims to use as scapegoats. When the manipulator does something wrong and is confronted, he or she will "project" his or guilt onto the victim in an effort to make the victim look like the responsible party.

• Feigning innocence: This technique can be used as part of a strategy of denial. Under questioning, the manipulator will "play innocent" by pretending that any violation was unintentional or that they were not the party who committed the violation.

• Feigning confusion: This technique can also be used as part of a strategy of denial. Under questioning, the manipulator will "play dumb" or pretend to be confused about the central point of the conflict or dispute. By creating confusion, the manipulator hopes to damage the confidence of his or victim.

● Peer pressure: By using claims, whether true or not, that the victim's friends, associates, or "everyone else" is doing something, the manipulator will put pressure on his victim to change his or her behavior or attitude.

Signs That You're Being Manipulated

We are all potentially susceptible to emotional manipulation by people who show characteristic signs of dark psychology.

A very easy example can be Victimization: it can occur in our everyday relationships with co-workers, bosses and supervisors, family members, and significant others.

Emotional manipulation can also occur in professional relationships with people we may regard as normally trustworthy—such as sales representatives, government officials, and other representatives of institutions such as medical facilities, banks, businesses, schools, and law firms.

Emotional predators share one common trait: They look for people who are conscientious, dependable, loyal, honest, and reliable. People with these character traits are the easiest to manipulate because all of the tricks in the manipulator's toolbox are designed specifically to take advantage of these emotional and psychological characteristics. More importantly, emotional predators lack empathy or morality. They do not regard their abuses as shocking or unacceptable; instead, they regard the overabundance of conscientious people as "job security" and a golden opportunity.

Emotional predators can be found in all walks of life. Over the course of their lives, they have learned how to adapt, blend in, and even achieve high levels of professional and financial success in the "straight world."

Remember that having a valid and legitimate expectation that people will be honest in their dealings with you means that you are a conscientious person. Although you occupy the superior position, emotional predators are highly skilled at exploiting this expectation and avoiding detection and/or punishment.

As we have seen, emotionally manipulative people use a wide variety of techniques and methods to gain power in relationships. What's more, the people you are closest to and most familiar with—people whom you should be able to trust the most—are in the best position to use emotional manipulation to exploit and take advantage of your trust. In fact, establishing trust and familiarity is one of the most important aspects of a successful effort to exploit someone's emotional vulnerability, then manipulate them either for personal gain or simply out of pure malice.

Of course, simply because this type of abuse has become common does not mean that you should automatically and necessarily regard all of your friends and trusted associates as predators and manipulators. Nor should you give into the temptation to regard being conscientious, law-abiding, and honest as a problem. However, victims of emotional manipulation are often unaware that they are being exploited and abused, so it is important to learn how to recognize the signs of manipulation.

Specific Examples of Emotional Manipulation

- insisting on meeting at certain locations: Manipulators may try to get the upper hand by insisting on a so-called "home court advantage," thereby forcing you to function in a less familiar and less comfortable environment that diminishes your personal negotiating power.

Examples:

o If you have a dispute with a professional acquaintance or colleague, they may insist on always meeting in their office or at a café or restaurant that is more difficult for you to travel to.

- Premature intimacy or closeness: The manipulator will immediately shower you with affection and reveal all sorts of intimate secrets.

Examples:

○   In a personal relationship, the manipulator may introduce themselves using phrases like, "No one has ever made me feel like this before. I know we were made for each other."

●   Managing conversations by always requiring you to speak first: In professional relationships, this is commonly used as a sales and negotiation technique to mine you for your information to make a more lucrative sale.

Examples:

○   A salesperson may say something like, "Rather than bore you with details about our products or services, why don't you tell me about yourself and how you think we can help you?"

●   Distorting or twisting facts: Whether in personal or professional relationships, manipulators will use conversational techniques to distort facts in an effort to make you doubt yourself and back down.

Example:

○   A manipulator may use a phrase like, "I understand how you feel. I'd be angry, too. But the truth is, I never made that comment. I don't think your memory of that conversation is accurate. I know what you really meant to say was that…"

- Intellectual bullying: An emotional manipulator may use an unnecessarily large volume of statistics, jargon, or other types of factual evidence to impose a sense of expertise.

- Bureaucratic bullying: This technique is similar to intellectual bullying. Unfortunately, this technique may indicate that someone is abusing their position of authority by insisting on placing as many obstacles, red tape, or other impediments in the way of what should be a straightforward resolution.

Example:

○ Such a person may make a statement such as, "I understand your concerns, but I would encourage you not to pursue this any further. You have a legitimate complaint, but the expenses and time required will likely cost more than you will get in return..

- Passive aggression

There are many examples of passive aggressive behavior in conversation in both personal and professional relationships to force you to back down to the predatory efforts of a manipulator.

Examples:

○ A manipulator may try to make you feel bad for voicing your concerns by saying something along the lines of, "I understand that you are voicing an important objection, but have ever stopped to consider what will happen to the rest of the team if you eventually get your way?"

• Insults and put-downs: Manipulators are good at following up rude or mean-spirited comments with sarcasm or some other attempt at humor to make it seem like they were joking.

Example:

○ "I know you really worked hard on that presentation. It's too bad you wasted your time, though. But, hey, no worries. I'm sure it will be great preparation when you interview for your position."

Chapter 6 Dealing With Manipulation in a Relationship

The culture romanticizes deceptive relations so much when talking about love that it can be hard to recognize them for what they are. We have lots of literature suggesting that genuine relationships are about fixation, that pure love is all-out, and that people who are infatuated have no boundaries or separate lives.

While many people romanticize the concept of a deceptive relationship, we have to realize that it is not real love. Sometimes it may trigger a dramatic storyline and tension that keeps the reader engaged, but there is no fun living through a deceptive relationship that is romantic.

You may have been warned of manipulating people and the fact that coercion and mistreatment are worrying; the facts are that being in a relationship of control and manipulation that never develops into ill-treatment can also be terrifying and dangerous. Just because somebody does not harm you physically does not mean you cannot feel pain from their actions yet.

Being dominated or put down by a partner can damage our faith, make us feel fearful of relationships in the future, and leave us feeling lost rather than comforted, with a variety of mental and emotional injuries with which we should not be burdened.

You may be familiar with the symptoms of a negative relationship. You might have met a partner, for instance, who required you to wear only certain clothing items or did not want you to visit your friends and family.

This person might want to know where you are going, what you are doing, and why you are just a couple of minutes late. Manipulators are frequently very anxious people, allowing nervous thoughts to pass through their brains and control their actions. We channel their intense fear and anxiety into hallucinations about what you might do if you are not around them. They are going to think about their worst fears and what you can do to damage them, so they are going to assume you are doing these things when you are not around.

Such things may spur them to hate you if you are not around. Sometimes it may seem flattering to have someone so concerned about you. You might think, "It is so sweet that they always want to know where I am, and I am safe," but it is not their intention when someone is going to take great steps to control you.

Unfortunately, they are not concerned about your well-being. Therefore, the manipulators are thinking, "I need to make sure I know where this person is at all times, so they do not do something that I do not approve of." Your presence is their assurance that you are not meeting their worst fears about the bad things that you are doing to them when you are not both of you together. In this case, they will not be addressing your needs. The manipulator behaves only to serve the interests of his own.

A manipulator will never tell you that but will only be worried about improving the way they look to you. They are always going to use this technique to make sure you feel guilty. They will make you feel guilty if you do not respond for 20 minutes, instead of admitting that it is acceptable for a person not always to write back immediately. They would view you as if you did something wrong or disrespectful to them because, at the time, you were not around your phone or too busy to answer first.

Marriage should feel better, not confining, scary, or distressing, and having an accomplice will make you happier, not more sorrowful. There will be hard times in life. Your mate may not be understood, and they may not understand you. On the way to making you stronger, these challenges should be pure obstacles. There shouldn't be a healthy relationship that continuously drains you and tears you down, making you feel constantly exhausted.

Signs of a Manipulative Relationship

Most of us have had terrible things happening in our lives— enough terrible things that the prospect of a hero sweeping us off our feet and protecting us from any problems for whatever remains of our lives can sound extremely tempting. For this reason, we are sometimes looking in the wrong places for security, empathy, and care.

Reconsider whether the support thoughts of your partner include stopping you from making your own decisions and living your own life. A partner who secures you by assuming responsibility for your maxed-out accounts, or perhaps speaking to a partner you have been struggling with, does not pay special attention to you; they are trying to make you have no choice but to put all your faith in them and no one else.

A true partner knows they cannot protect you and what it holds from everyday life — they can just support when you need them. If you run into a money-related issue at some point, a trusted partner can help you pray an overabundance of unopened bills— give help, but do not take control of the situation. They will not take your passwords or insist that only a small amount of money per month be allowed until you have paid off all of your current debt. A true partner is going to offer help yet realize you need to manage your problems.

One common manipulative technique of relationship is to make us feel guilty when we see friends and family members. If we imagine someone trying to cut off their partner from their emotionally supportive network, we envision something similar to the contemptible husband in a movie made for TV that threatens his better half that she will never talk to her closest friend again. Nevertheless, deceptive spouses can also inconspicuously isolate you from your support network.

A shrewdly manipulative person will not outwardly discourage you from seeing your family because it can be an obvious sign that you should be running in the opposite direction. We will make the coercion more subtle, rather than slowly dragging you out of your life, rather than an outright ban. If your partner can convince you to apologize for an action that you know you have not done wrongly and that you are doing, your manipulative partner will realize that he or she can force you to do whatever they want you to do.

Each time you go out with your buddies, your partner can sulk until you blow off other friends just to save the tension. Perhaps your partner will make negative remarks about your loved ones until you begin to believe that the thoughts, they have about these people are valid.

You may even have a hobby or an event you enjoy trying to get your manipulator to stop doing it. They will make sure that you know that your interest is idiotic and will ridicule you until you give it up.

The scrutiny of a controlling partner may not always appear as such. It can be framed reasonably and rationally, implying that your partner is just trying to help you. They might even tell you they are trying to help you.

At school, they will research your decisions. Some of their sentences may include: "Why do you choose to use it for your presentation? You are not thinking about what the boss will think? They are going to question your spending habits and how you are going to buy things with questions like, "Did you have to buy another shirt?" Manipulators are going to spin their words, so it is not clear that the choices you make are wrong, but a seed of doubt and insecurity is being planted.

All partners, however, examine each other periodically. Our loved ones are still supposed to look for us, and sometimes we need others to help us make choices or point out bad habits. Remember, always test this person's true purpose and find out why they had wanted you to change your actions.

Sometimes a manipulator may ask for access to your personal belongings in a relationship, but they will not grant you the same rights. We may know all your secrets, but we rarely trust you.

They are not just less likely to share, and they are not helping you.

This type of behavior demonstrates that the other person dominates. Your partner does not reserve the right to search your emails or texts or asking for your passwords because they say they are concerned that you may be cheating. There is a distinction between having insider facts and having healthy independence from your partner, and when you are in a relationship with someone, you do not have to surrender that.

Every so often, sincere couples healing from a disaster would require the weakened spouse to view the messages of each other as a form of transparency. But, if this is not an agreement you have worked out directly with your partner, it is incorrect.

By emotional influence, coercion is all about influencing the way someone else thinks and acts. Coercion is veiled with emotion, or at least what appears to be a sort of empathy. Most of the time, this is a calculated attempt by the manipulator concerned to relate to the victim.

We must recognize the impact it has had on us to overcome this manipulation completely. If you want a healthy relationship with someone, we must look at all the ways we have been affected by their relationship. It may be the first sign that there is a manipulative relationship if that impact is negative.

Most manipulative people have four standard attributes: they know the weaknesses.

They use your vulnerabilities against you.

They persuade you to surrender something of yourself to serve them through their quick plots.

If a controller triumphs in manipulating you, he is likely to repeat the crime until the mistreatment is stopped.

They are going to have a lot of different reasons for keeping you around and controlling you. One might just be because a past relationship damages them. We may have confidence issues that have made it difficult for them to be transparent and consider other partners. This situation can make them feel like they need to manipulate you to keep you loyal to them. Many partners could be lonely people who are desperate for love and attention. You will stop at nothing to make sure you stick around, even if that means bribery, whether you feel like you are going to take that path or are afraid you are going to abandon them. You may also just want practical things from you, such as financial support, or your shared house, a car, and other benefits that are not connected to you as a person they love, but rather the life you choose to live. These are some of the most dangerous manipulators and are as normal as the others.

Chapter 7 Persuasion Methods

What is Neuro Linguistic Programing?

- N: neurology–linked to the brain and nervous system

- L: linguistics–usage and impact of the language that we use

- P: programming–activities used to accomplish the expected objectives.

Neuro-linguistic programming (NLP) is a psychological approach involving the analysis and application of strategies used by successful individuals to achieve a specific goal. It applies to different results, feelings, words, and behavior patterns learned through experience. NLP supporters believe that all human actions are optimistic. Therefore, if a plan fails or the bad happens, then the event is neither good nor bad— it provides more useful information.

How NLP Works

If you are just coming across this topic for the first time, NLP may appear or seem like magic or hypnosis.

When a person is undergoing therapy, this topic digs deep into the unconscious mind of the patient and filters through different layers of beliefs and the person's approach or perception of life to deduce the early childhood experiences that are responsible for a behavioral pattern.

In NLP, it is believed that everyone has the resources that are needed for positive changes in their own lives. The technique adopted here is meant to help in facilitating these changes.

Usually, when NLP is taught, it is done in a pyramidal structure. However, the most advanced techniques are left for those multi-thousand-dollar seminars. An attempt to explain this complicated subject is to state that the NLPer (as those who use NLP will often call themselves) is always paying keen attention to the person they are working on/with.

Usually, there is a large majority of NLPers that are therapists and they are very likely to be well-meaning people. They achieve their aims by paying attention to those subtle cues like the movement of the eyes, flushing of the skin, dilation of the pupil and subtle nervous tics. It is easy for an NLP user to quickly determine the following:

The side of the brain that the person uses predominantly.

The sense (smell, sight, etc.) that is more dominant in a person's brain.

The way the person's brain stores and makes use of information (the NLPer can deduce all this from the person's eye movement).

When they are telling a lie or concocting information.

When the NLP user has successfully gathered all this information, they begin to mimic the client in a slow and subtle manner by not only taking on their body language, but also by imitating their speech and mannerisms, so that they begin to talk with the language patterns that are aimed at targeting the primary senses of the client. They will typically fake the social cues that will easily make someone let their guard down so that they become very open and suggestible.

For example, when a person's sense of sight is their most dominant sense, the NLPer will use a language that is very laden with visual metaphors to speak with them. They will say things like: "do you see what I am talking about?" or "why not look at it this way?" For a person that has a more dominant sense of hearing, he will be approached with an auditory language like: "listen to me" or "I can hear where you're coming from."

To create a rapport, the NLPer mirrors the body language and the linguistic patterns of the other person. This rapport is a mental and physiological state which a human being gets into when they lose guard of their social senses. It is done when they begin to feel like the other person who they are conversing with is just like them.

Once the NLPer have achieved this rapport, they will take charge of the interaction by leading it in a mild and subtle manner. Thanks to the fact that they have already mirrored the other person, they will now begin to make some subtle changes in order to gain a certain influence on the behavior of the person. This is also combined with some similar subtle language patterns which lead to questions and a whole phase of some other techniques.

At this point, the NLPer will be able to tweak and twist the person to whichever direction they so desire. This only happens if the other person can't deduce that there is something going on because they assume everything that is occurring is happening organically or that they have given consent to everything.

In NLP, there is the belief in the need for the perfection of the nature of human creation, so every client is encouraged to recognize the sensitivity of the senses and make use of them in responding to specific problems. As a matter of fact, NLP also holds the belief that it is possible for the mind to find cures to diseases and sicknesses.

What is done in Neuro-Linguistic Programming?

Dissociation

Have you been in a scenario where you were feeling bad? Perhaps you've experienced something that gets you down every time you think it. Or maybe you're getting nervous in some work situations where you have to speak out in public. Perhaps when you want to meet the "special person" you've had your focus on, you get nervous. While these feelings of shyness, nervousness, or sadness tend to be inevitable or relentless, NLP dissociation strategies can be of immense help.

Content Reframing

Use this strategy when you feel pessimistic or powerless in a situation. Reframing can take any negative case and inspire you by having something optimistic about the nature of the experience. You own the right to do whatever you want when you want to. And from this relationship, you have learned valuable lessons that will facilitate you to have better relationships with other people. These are all examples of how a scenario is reframed. You give yourself a different experience of that by reframing the sense of the breakup.

Anchoring Yourself

Anchoring derives from the Russian psychologist Ivan Pavlov who worked with dogs by continually ringing a bell while the dogs fed. Upon numerous bell rings, he found that by ringing the bell at any time, he could see the dogs salivate, even if there was no food in the pot. It created a neural connection called a conditioned response between the bell and the salivation behavior. You can use those kinds of "anchors" stimulus-response yourself! Anchoring yourself helps you associate any desired positive emotional response to a specific phrase or feeling.

Rapport (Getting Other People to Like You)

It is a simple collection of NLP strategies, but they have the power to help almost everyone get along with you. There are many ways to build relationships with other people. NLP comes as one of the fastest and most effective ways. This technique involves a deliberate mirroring of the body language, tone of voice, and phrases of another person. Individuals prefer individuals who are as they are. When unconsciously mirroring the other person, the brain sets off "mirror neurons," receptors of pleasure inside the mind that make people feel like someone imitating them.

Influence and Persuasion

Much of the NLP's research is committed to helping people eradicate negative emotions, restricting attitudes, bad habits, conflict, and more, another aspect of NLP is dedicated to how to manipulate others ethically and convince them.

One mentor in the area, Milton H. Erickson, was a man named. Erickson was a psychiatrist who also researched the subconscious mind using the hypnotherapy (the real, scientific stuff not the dumb hypnosis of entertainment you see in stage shows).

Erickson was so adept at hypnosis, and he developed a way of speaking to other people's subconscious minds without hypnosis. In everyday conversations, he could hypnotize people anytime, anywhere. The Ericksonian form of hypnosis has become known as "Conversational Hypnosis." It's a potent tool that can be used not only to manipulate and convince others but also to help people resolve fears, restrict perceptions, conflict, and more without their consciousness. It is particularly useful when you get across to people who would otherwise be resilient if they know (think young kids who don't want to hear).

Neuro-Linguistic Programing and Communication

Neuro linguistic Programming, or NLP, has become a popular way of talking about human thought and communication for many non-psychologists. It's a version of Popular Psychology. While it's far beyond the reach of our discussion to criticize NLP (because such criticism would cover several issues), you must know a few things about the communication and non-verbal skills and strategies, that is supposed to be efficient and being promoted by both reputable and untrustworthy teachers and so-called master practitioners. Unlike mainstream or popular areas such as linguistics, neuroscience, or psychology, which have their basis in academic research using controlled studies, NLP tends to focus on "what works" and derives many of its methods from other disciplines in practice. So, while several non-verbal communication NLP methods and declarations may have strong research support, it is also likely that some of the techniques and arguments are not validated correctly in controlled study environments.

The message for casual non-verbal communication students is that reading NLP content may introduce you to some excellent and right concepts from fields such as psychology and linguistics. Still, it will also expose you to ideas and assumptions that are not validated or may be invalid. The problem is that you are not going to be able to assess what is valid and what isn't by relying on NLP literature and courses. NLP does not provide a unified theory— it's more of a hodge-podge of useful things.

To explain the range of things that some practitioners include in NLP: the principle or principles are borrowed from linguistics, certainly a valid and agreed way of looking at communication. On the other extreme is the hypnotic regression of past life, which is far outside the limits of accepted scientific practice. Both are deemed part of the NLP. Then, to clarify, marketing claims and professionals who say they can show you how to tell you when people are lying by looking at their eye movements and how to seduce women by applying NLP techniques can be found.

All this to explain why we don't have nonverbal behavioral elements that are explicitly taken from NLP and not present in more traditional, well-researched, and regulated fields

The concept found within the NLP is that professional communicators use standard verbal and non-verbal communication techniques to establish interaction with others. Such approaches are based on an understanding of the internal sensory interpretation structures that are used by people to interpret and make sense of their experiences. An in-depth NLP Training will try to ensure that you gain a highly evolved ability to recognize this very subtle form of communication and respond to it. That's because it is one of the necessary skills that much of the' magic' of NLP depends upon. Applying NLP to communicate expertly or to develop excellent relations, or coaching someone in personal development or using most of the well-known NLP techniques requires you to have a unique ability to recognize nonverbal communication.

Chapter 8 Hypnosis and Hypnotherapy

Hypnosis or hypnotherapy is a state that is trance-like where a person's focus is heightened as well as their concentration. Hypnosis is done with the assistance of a therapist that uses verbal repetitions and mental pictures. When a person is put under hypnosis, they normally feel relaxed, calm and are open to suggestions.

Therapists have used hypnosis to help individuals gain control over behaviors that are undesirable. In dealing with anxiety and pain, hypnosis has also been found to be helpful. Although a person is relaxed and more open-minded to receive various suggestions, it is important to know that a person doesn't lose control over their behavior.

Why is hypnosis done?

Therapists say that hypnosis is an excellent way to cope with anxiety and stress. For instance, if someone is supposed to go for a medical procedure that they are anxious and stressed about, hypnosis can help calm them before the procedure. There are various conditions where hypnosis is used. These may include:

Pain control – if a person is suffering from chronic pains from cancer, childbirth, joints, headaches among others, hypnosis may help in bearing the pain.

Hot flashes – when a woman is going through menopause, she will experience hot flashes that are uncomfortable most of the time. Hypnosis has been known to help with the discomfort of hot flashes.

Behavior change – some people may find themselves having behaviors that are undesirable. Such include bed-wetting, insomnia, eating disorders, among others. The use of hypnosis has been known to help in transforming these undesirable behaviors.

Side effects of cancer treatment – during cancer treatment, patients go through chemotherapy and radiation treatment. These forms of treatments leave the patient with undesirable side effects. The use of hypnosis helps cancer patients deal with these effects and cope with the treatment.

Mental health conditions – many people suffer from various mental health issues such as post-traumatic stress, anxiety, phobias, among many more. The uses of hypnosis help a person deal with these conditions and bring relief.

What are the risks of hypnosis?

When hypnosis is done by a trained therapist or a medical practitioner, it is considered a safe addition and alternative treatment. However, in people with serious mental health issues, hypnosis may not be the best method to use. There are various reactions to hypnosis. However, these reactions are rare and they include:

The person may feel dizzy after therapy

Experience slight headaches

After therapy, a person may feel drowsy

A person can be distressed or anxious

In rare cases, hypnosis can create false memories

Three Stages of Hypnosis

Hypnosis is a process that involves the deep body and mind relaxation. Before we get to the various hypnosis stages, it is important to first understand how hypnosis works or the process of hypnotherapy.

Getting ready – every hypnotherapy session with a qualified therapist must be carried out in a relaxed, safe and calm environment where there are no interruptions of any kind. There is usually a preliminary discussion between the therapist and the person to be hypnotized. This is usually done to establish if the person has had prior hypnotism sessions and their experiences as well as trying to establish the problem one needs working on.

Most of the problems usually include a behavior or thoughts a person needs to balance or completely changed. For instance, a person may be struggling with bed-wetting; this behavior with the help of hypnosis is addressed and changed.

A skilled therapist should gather as much information as possible during the preliminary talk. This is important so that he may work on the best technique for the particular person and problem. The pattern most therapists use during the session is loose. It follows:

Preparing and screening a client

Inducting a client to an altered state consciousness state

Deepening the trance state that opens suggestibility

Posthypnotic suggestions. This is where advice is given regarding the problem the therapist worked on.

Induction – in a typical hypnotherapy session, the initial 15 minutes are for helping the client relax their mind and body. This stage is referred to as the induction stage. It involves helping a person to enter into a light state of trance by the use of relaxation techniques that work on the mind and body.

Gradually, the person is encouraged to relax their muscles and mind. This technique is aimed at ridding a person of any tension and releasing anxiety. The therapist focuses on instructing the client to slow and control their breathing. This is also to help relax and distract the conscious mind so that a person focuses on the subconscious mind. Because of many methods of induction, it is important for the therapist to understand their client and apply a method that works for them.

Deepening a trance – this stage is where the subconscious mind is made ready to be more receptive to suggestions or new behavior. Once the mind accepts new thought patterns, a change in behavior follows. To deepen the trance, some therapists may opt to continue reinforcing the induction method used. The method can be accompanied by visualization techniques that are very deep to increase the trance. A qualified therapist knows that it is important for a person to be deeply altered in consciousness before starting hypnotic suggestions.

Now that you know how hypnosis works, it is important to understand the three stages to hypnotism.

Stage 1 – Hypnoidal State

This is the stage of light induction. At this stage, the person is encouraged to relax and have an internal focus. This stage is light and is characterized by the fluttering of the eyes of the person.

Stage 2 – Cataleptic State

This is the stage where the therapist moves to deepen the trance state. To know if a person is in this state, their eyes move from one side to the other.

Stage 3 – Somnambulistic State

This is the deepest stage in a trance. This is evidenced by the rolling up and down of eyes. This is the stage where suggestions are given and received at a subconscious level and the person in some cases may not remember hearing them.

Applications for Hypnosis

Hypnosis has been known to have existed for as long as records have been able to show. According to the American Society for Clinical Hypnosis (ASCH), the use of modern clinical hypnotherapy goes back to the late 1700s. Since 1958, the use of hypnotherapy as a form of reliable therapy and tremendously increased.

Hypnotherapy has found use in the modern world in different ways.

Hypnosis is used in various ways from mental health conditions to psychological and physical conditions. It is used on people suffering from chronic pain, depression, in sudden and acute illnesses, among others. Most health professionals nowadays recommend the use of hypnosis to treat their clients facing different conditions. Some of the uses of hypnosis include:

Treatment of phobias and fears

Unreasonable irrational fear or phobia of anything can be treated through the use of hypnotism. Many people struggle with phobias on a daily basis causing them not to function normally. Some of the fears that paralyze people are fear of spiders or arachnophobia, fear of enclosed spaces or claustrophobic, fear of heights, snakes, flying or agoraphobia; the fear of leaving home. A hypnotherapist will work with a patient while under hypnotism to try and identify the reasons for the fears and work on finding solutions to them.

Stopping smoking

There are people that want to stop their habit of smoking but it becomes very difficult. Most smokers attempt several times to quit smoking and find themselves falling back. Regardless of how committed a smoker is to cease smoking, it is not easy and they may need help to do so. A hypnotherapist may be able to help them. In a relaxed environment, the therapist works on understanding the various stress factors in the life of the client that may be causing fall back to smoking every time they stop. A therapist will go to the subconscious mind to find these reasons and make suggestions on how to stop. Once the subconscious mind has received the suggestions, it is then possible for the person to change their behavior by addressing the stress factors.

Weight loss

Many people struggle with weight loss and often feel they have lost the battle with food. With a qualified hypnotherapist, a person can learn more about their relationship with food. They also learn why they have no control over food and how to overcome their cravings. Through hypnosis, a therapist can suggest ways to overcome the destructive behavior and have a healthy relationship with food.

Boosting Confidence

There are many people that suffer from low self-esteem issues. To gain their confidence back, such people may require assistance. Most people lose confidence because they can seem to embrace their good qualities. A therapist can help such a person find their confidence by tapping on their best qualities that are subconsciously hidden.

Anesthesiology during surgery

There are cases where a surgeon may hire a hypnotherapist to supplement medical anesthesia. In some extremely rare cases, hypnotherapy has been used solely as an anesthetic during a surgical procedure. Some procedures that surgeons have used hypnotherapy include the removal of gall bladder, cesarean, hysterectomy, and amputation. There are patients that have sensitiveness and allergies of chemicals used in anesthesia. However, they can still benefit from health-improving and life-saving procedures through the use of hypnotherapy.

Hypnosis has been credited with improving the lives of many people. For cognitive-behavioral therapy, hypnotism has been known to help many patients transform their thoughts and in effect changing their outward behaviors for better.

Hypnotherapy

This is a way of using hypnosis as a technique in psychotherapy. In this area, it is used in a way that it helps a patient, or a subject get rid of the things that are constantly troubling them. This is most commonly used in cases where the other methods of self-control fail to take effect.

When a patient is dealing with a licensed psychologist or physician, the doctor might make the patient go through a form of hypnotherapy, if the patient is willing, to enable them to treat the post-traumatic stress, eating disorders, compulsive gambling, anxiety, sleep disorders or depression that is constantly plaguing the patient.

A certified hypnotherapist may also be able to help a patient by treating issues like weight management. However, it is important to note that certified hypnotherapists are not physicians or psychologists, so all they can do is help you go through your journey to reaching the hypnotic state. The hypnotherapist cannot possibly help you cure ailments that are more serious.

Make sure that the person you have chosen to work with has already been certified to give you the services you require, regardless of whether you have chosen a physician or a hypnotherapist.

The graph below explains the process of smoking cessation:

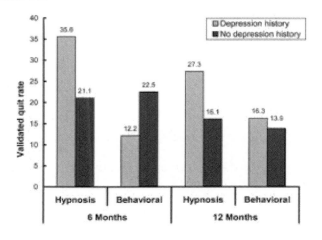

Carrying out hypnotherapy is done in different ways and all of them have a different degree of success depending on whatever the participant's issue is. Below are some of the known forms of conducting hypnotherapy:

• In cognitive behavioral hypnotherapy behavioral hypnotherapy is combined with clinical hypnosis.

• Hypnoanalysis is a type of hypnosis used to assist people who are dealing with fears and phobias. It is also known as the age regression hypnotherapy.

• Ericksonian hypnotherapy is used to help those that are dealing with addictions.

• Hypnotherapy in dealing with the control of habits

• Hypnotherapy in dealing with the management of pain in people dealing with severe and/or chronic pain

• Hypnotherapy in assisting in psychological therapy for people that are already dealing with it

• Hypnotherapy in assisting with relaxation

• Hypnotherapy used for certain diseases of the skin.

• Soothing patients those are anxious about undergoing a surgical process with hypnotherapy.

• Boosting the performance of athletes before they begin competition with the use of hypnotherapy.

• Using hypnotherapy to help with weight loss

Chapter 9 Brainwashing

What is Brain Washing?

In the early 1950s, Brainwashing was coined by journalist Edward Hunter who wanted to describe the Chinese Communists ' efforts to control the minds and to think processes of the Chinese people after their takeover in 1949. Brainwashing is a method of controlling or influencing the personal beliefs, thoughts, attitudes, or actions of people themselves to make them believe what they had previously considered being false. The word "brainwashing" originated from its Nao, the Chinese term, which means "washing the brain." Brainwashing is a method by which a person or group makes use of strict austerity measures to influence others to the will of the manipulator. But where does he stop honest persuasion and start brainwashing? Today, there are many forms of persuasion employed, especially in politics. For instance, a simple way to persuade a crowd to follow your instructions is first to state a few things that cause a' yes' response, then add items that are actual realities, and finally, recommend what you want them to do.

Methods

• In psychology, the brainwashing study often referred to as the reform of thought, falls into the "social influence" sphere. Every minute of every day, social influence happens. It's the set of ways people can change perceptions, values, and actions of other people. The enforcement approach, for example, attempts to bring about a change in a person's behavior and is not concerned about his ethics or values. It is the strategy of "Just do this."

• Persuasion, on the other side, points for a change of attitude, or "Do it because it will make you feel good/happy/healthy/successful."

• The method of education (which is called the "propaganda method" when you don't believe in what's being taught) goes for the gold of social-influence, attempting to affect a transformation in the person's ideas, along the lines of "Do it because you know it's right."

Techniques That Are Used in Brain Washing

Chanting and Singing

Chanting mantras is an essential feature of many religions, notably Buddhism and Hinduism, and nearly every church has some form of hymn-singing adoration. As each church member chants or sings the same words, their voices merge into one song, creating a strong sense of unity and collective identity. That, along with established singing effects such as lowered heart rate and relaxation, could cast the experience of community worship into a positive light. Increased suggestibility is a feature of such a state, and failure to maintain the trance is often followed by the punishment inflicted on cults, ensuring continuous enforcement of ultra-conformist behavior. Psychologists Linda Dubrow-Marshall and Steve Eichel have researched how being exposed to repetitive and sustained hypnotic inductions can affect the ability of the convert to make decisions and interpret new information.

Love Bombing

Cults want to reinforce the feeling that the outside world is threatening and gravely mistaken. In comparison, they also use "love bombing" to make themselves look accommodating. Love bombing means showering with lavish new or prospective hires and displaying attention and affection. The term has probably originated with either the Children of God or the Church of Unification, but can now be practiced to several different organizations. It is a phenomenon of social psychology that we feel strongly compelled to reciprocate other people's kind acts and kindness. It is, so the counterfeit affection, encouragement, and goodwill shown towards initiates by existing cult members are processed to create a growing sense of debt, obligation, and guilt. Margaret Singer called this an essential character of the cult, useful because it's precisely companionship and validation that many new cult recruits are searching for.

The psychologist Edgar Schein claims that people are triggered into a cult through a process of "unfreezing and refreezing. A new cult member starts to reject his old view of the world during the unfreezing stage and becomes open to the ideas of the cults. The cult solidifies this new perspective during refreezing. Schein mentions to love bombing as a critical point of refreezing — recruits who accept the philosophy of cults are rewarded with hugs and compliments but shunned when they ask too many skeptic questions.

Barratrous Abuse

Most cults hire attorneys to prosecute anyone who criticizes them publicly, no matter how trivial the criticism may be. Of course, the cult can usually afford to lose the lawsuits, while ex-cult members are often insolvent after giving the organization's life. Consequently, many ex-cultists are unable to mount an effective legal counterattack. Moreover, due to the ever-present threat of legal action, mainstream journalists are afraid to criticize cult or reference religious material.

Fatigue and Sleep Deprivation

Amway, a multi-level marketing company, has been charged with depriving its distributors of sleep during weekend-long events. It happened because they were including non-stop seminars lasting until the early morning hours, with only brief interludes during which musicians play loud music with lights flashing. A cultivation strategy that is sometimes used in combination with sleep deprivation includes advising participants to adopt special diets that contain low protein levels and other essential nutrients. As a result, the members of the cults will always feel tired, making them powerless to resist the dictates of religious doctrine.

Activity Pedagogy

How does a teacher motivate their students to follow ethical behavior and conformism? The solution is often to integrate some sort of physical exercise or sport into their teaching. Involved in jumping on the spot or running around, and consequently tired, children are less likely to argue or cause trouble. By acknowledging this phenomenon, several cults aimed to have members occupied as a means of control with an endless series of tiring activities. For example, some believe cults such as Dahn Yoga are just physical exercise programs on the surface. Mass sporting events like calisthenics in stadiums in Russia were a recognizable feature of the Soviet system, and historians associate them with the repressive state apparatus. What distinguishes activity pedagogy from mere sports is that the increased mood and group identity experienced after physical activity will be used by a regime or cult to introduce ideological views that could otherwise be met with skepticism. Fatigue by exercise is yet another manner in which the barriers of people can be worn away as a means to enable them to embrace dubious ideas.

The difference between Brainwashing Techniques

Cults will also use the following methods to exploit that isn't usually used in the brainwashing techniques mentioned above:

• Hypnotherapy

• The manipulation-double agendas-the target assumes they get one thing, but the truth is they get something else

• Love bombing-showering new members with love and affection to make them feel special.

• Childhood games to induce age regression and promote compliance

• No questioning or criticism of leadership is allowed

• Young participants are usually accompanied by more experienced members and are not given time to think alone

• Cult promotes financial participation as a way of encouraging psychological involvement

- Childhood games to cause age regression and promote obedience • No queries or criticism of leadership is allowed

- New members are usually preceded by more experienced members and are not given time to think alone

- Cult encourages financial engagement as a means of encouraging psychological commitment

Chapter 10 How to Protect Yourself against Emotional Predator

Let's start by looking at an example of typical Emotional Predator behavior that includes omitting relevant facts to hide the truth, ignoring rules, denying facts, being indignant and bullying when called on bad behavior, blaming their target, being hypocritical, refusing to inconvenience themselves or change, being indifferent to their negative impact on others, playing the victim, and manipulating emotions with melodramatic tones and words.

There is no "one size fits all" approach to dealing with an Emotional Predator in your life.. This means that no single strategy or tactic can be guaranteed to neutralize every Emotional Predator. Learning how to protect you is a process of trial and error. And trial and error doesn't work when we demand perfect results each time. So let yourself off the hook of perfectionism. When a tactic doesn't work as you'd hoped, it's not a failure, it's a learning opportunity.

Some of the ways to protect yourself can be easy to understand but difficult to put into practice and internalize, others harder to understand. Make notes in the margins, on the Table of Contents or on the blank pages at the beginning or end. Create your own table of contents so you can find things that are particularly important to you.

Identify Emotional Predators

The first step in protecting yourself from Emotional Predators is to recognize them behind their camouflage.

As you read about the behaviors, tactics and traits of Emotional Predators, you may recognize some of them in yourself and worry that you may be one of them. We all can share some of the behaviors that distinguish Emotional Predators from others, and under stress we can temporarily regress to some of those more primitive ways (and many teenagers seem to temporarily regress that way as part of a natural developmental phase). And as we'll see, we also can choose to selectively adopt some Emotional Predator tactics to defend ourselves from Emotional Predators.

Emotional Predators exhibit a pervasive and enduring pattern of behavior and perception, not a selective, temporary use of tactics. That's why it can take repeated observations over time and examining documented history to determine whether someone is an Emotional Predator, or just a decent person temporarily regressed under stress or selectively resorting to defensive tactics.

You don't become an Emotional Predator by selectively using some of the clever or even devious Emotional

Predator tactics to protect yourself and your loved ones. You can choose to use the same tactics without sharing the same traits and nature. Selectively playing an Emotional Predator's game better than she does in order to protect yourself, and with concern for the negative impact on innocent people, is very different from the Emotional Predator's pervasive use of tactics to use and abuse others for her own ends without regard to the costs imposed on others.

And Emotional Predators lack insight into themselves. They're deeply delusional about who they are and, in particular, how they impact others. Although they can fake it using the jargon of psychotherapy, they're not truly introspective. Recognizing Emotional Predator behaviors and tactics in yourself, suggests that you're more introspective than they are.

Be Flexible about how you define yourself

Emotional Predators seek out emotionally reactive people and harness their emotional reactions to control them. But a strategically responsive person can regain control and power and is a less appealing target. Your emotional reactions control you. You control your strategic responses.

Although it's natural to want to change an Emotional Predator, don't underestimate the power of changing yourself. Knowing yourself better than she knows you is essential, but more powerful protection comes when you're willing to change yourself. And you're the only person you can change. You can't change who she is. You can, however, change who you are to fortify your defenses, build immunity and improve your responses. And by changing yourself and how you respond, you can influence her behaviors. Later we'll look at specific strategies to influence Emotional Predators' behaviors, but don't confuse that with changing who they are.

Avoid and Disengage when possible

The wizards are right. Have the wisdom to run from Emotional Predators whenever you can. When you identify an Emotional Predator in your world, the best thing to do is avoid engaging with them. That's easiest when she isn't targeting you and you're observing her from the sidelines. In that situation, just steer clear and avoid involvement. This should be done politely and without any hint that you see anything wrong or negative about her. You certainly shouldn't explain to an Emotional Predator the real reason you're moving away. If she asks, some version of the old line from dating of "It's not you, it's me" is usually the best approach. Be too busy. Make vague circumstances the "bad cop" that forces you to decline engaging with her.

As you move away from an Emotional Predator, don't explain or justify, just state your unavailability in the briefest way possible. "I have too much going on," without being drawn into listing and justifying what else you have going on, is usually enough. Particularly after you've already said you aren't available, often the most powerful response to further inquiry is no response at all. Silence can speak loudly and clearly (and uses the Emotional Predator tactic of passive-aggression for protection). Be as invisible as you can, showing fear or vulnerability, joy or excitement, satisfaction or disappointment. Show no emotion at all, because your emotions are what an Emotional Predator feeds on and will try to manipulate.

If you find yourself already engaged with an Emotional Predator, the best thing to do is disengage. But that may not always be possible. If the Emotional Predator is in your family or at your work, you may need to, or you may choose to, stay engaged.

Be Strategic when you do engage

The strategy of avoiding and disengaging may not be available or practical in your situation, particularly if the Emotional Predator is part of your family or at your work. If you must, or if you choose to, remain involved with an Emotional Predator (you have children together, for example), it's vital to be smart and strategic, and use effective tactics, to protect yourself and your loved ones and restore the balance of power. Every strategy and tactic for dealing with an Emotional Predator, including disengaging, aims to re-balance power and restore control.

Many of the tactics for managing involvement with an Emotional Predator can be summed up as playing the Emotional Predator's game better than she does and setting your own rules of engagement. Don't bring a knife to a gun fight. Remember, playing her game better than she plays it doesn't make you an Emotional Predator. The tactics themselves may look the same and an uninformed observer may not readily distinguish between offensive and defensive uses, but there's a world of difference.

Control Information

Controlling information is central to any strategy for protecting yourself. An Emotional Predator will carefully control the information she lets out, telling affirmative lies and distortions as well as lying by omission. This makes it important for you to mine all sources of information to get the facts and fill in what she's left out. Penetrate her facade by gathering information about her abusive, deceptive and manipulative behaviors and reality.

An Emotional Predator also will relentlessly try to mine you for information about you, particularly for information about what's emotionally important to you, what you hold near and dear to your heart, your core beliefs and values. So learn to play her hiding game better than she does by controlling the information you let out. The less she knows about you the better. Don't say what you want to say, say what will be strategically smart to say.

Like a good card player, remember that misleading your opponent is central to a good outcome. When an Emotional Predator thinks you care about things that are unimportant to you (and visa versa), she'll attack you where you're immune and not attack you where you're vulnerable. You can strategically mislead her both by withholding accurate information about you and by releasing inaccurate information. Although strategically faking an emotional display can put an Emotional Predator off balance and misdirect her attention, this tactic should be used sparingly and only by the theatrically inclined. Unless you're a good actor, it's probably better to remain emotionally invisible.

Types, Sources and Direction of Information Flow

Managing the flow of information between you and an Emotional Predator, and with third parties, is part of almost all the strategies for protecting yourself. There are three types of information: information about you, about the Emotional Predator and about the situation. In addition, information moves in two directions: you acquire it and you release it.

You can acquire information from three sources: from yourself, from the Emotional Predator and from third parties (which includes independent records). And you can release information to any of three audiences: to yourself, to the Emotional Predator or to third parties. Particularly when releasing information, but also when acquiring it, involve third parties with caution. Through ignorance or intention, third parties may or may not be trustworthy. Some could be helpful, others could be oblivious, still others could be enlisted now or in the future as Emotional Predator helpers or patsies.

This may sound more complex than it is. The bottom line is that effective protection from Emotional Predators involves controlling the information you reveal and acquire, considering what that information is, from whom it's acquired and to whom it's shared. Managing all the different types of information and the directions they flow is a central part of an effective defense, but controlling the information you let out about yourself, particularly about your emotions, is essential. If you wear your heart on your sleeve and let your emotional states be visible, there's little hope of effective protection. Common therapy admonitions to be open and honest and share your feelings are a disaster if you follow them with an Emotional Predator.

Chapter 11 Tips to read and analyze people

Take a moment to imagine a time when the sight of someone sent a chill down your spine. You may not have known why, but you were simply uncomfortable around the person that you were facing. Despite your best attempts to identify the reasoning behind your problem, you found that there was no particular reason that you could discern. The only thing you knew was that you were the only thing afraid of the person in front of you and had no idea how to overcome them.

There was a very good reason for this guttural reaction—your instincts were telling you that something about the other person was not right. You didn't need to know specifics, and all that mattered to you was that your reactions were accurate. This is because all these guttural reactions must do keep you alive. So long as that is managed, your instincts did their job.

There are limitless reasons that being able to rationally understand what is going on in someone else's mind is critical, even if you already have a decent gut reaction. Ultimately, when you can analyze someone calmly and consciously be aware of why you are uncomfortable or what is putting you on-edge, you are better prepared to cope with the problem at hand. This is because you can act rationally. You can strategize on how to better react in the most conducive manner that will allow you to succeed in the situation.

This means that in the modern world, when things are very rarely life or death situations, making an effort to switch to responding rationally and consciously is almost always the best bet. You will be able to tell when someone is setting off your alarm bells because they seem threatening, or because they seem deceptive. You will be able to find out what the problem is to respond appropriately.

Why Analyze People

Analyzing people is something that is utilized by several people in different capacities. The most basic reason you may decide that you wish to analyze someone is to simply understand them. When you have an in-built technique of understanding others, you will discover that having a cognitive instead of an emotional connection is critical to establishing a true connection with someone else's mind.

Consider for a moment that you are trying to land a deal with a very important client. You know that the deal is critical if you hope to keep your job and possibly even get a promotion, but you also know that it is going to be a difficult task to manage. If you can read someone else, you can effectively allow yourself the ability to truly know what is going on in their mind.

Think about it—you will be able to tell if the client is uncomfortable and respond accordingly. You will be able to tell if the client is being deceptive or withholding something—and respond accordingly. You can tell if the client is uninterested, feeling threatened, or even just annoyed with your attempts to sway him or her, and you can then find out how to reply.

When you can understand the mindset of someone else, you can self-regulate. You can fine-tune your behaviors to guarantee that you will be persuasive. You can make sure that your client feels comfortable by being able to adjust your behavior to find out what was causing the discomfort in the first place.

Beyond just being able to self-regulate, being able to read other people is critical in several other situations as well. If you can read someone else, you can protect yourself from any threats that may arise. If you can read someone else, you can simply understand their position better. You can find out how to persuade or manipulate the other person. You can get people to do things that they would otherwise avoid.

Ultimately, being able to analyze other people has so many critical benefits that it is worthwhile to be able to do so. Developing this skill set means that you will be more in touch with the feelings of those around you, allowing you to assert that you have a higher emotional intelligence simply because you come to understand what emotions look like. You will be able to identify your own emotions through self-reflection and to learn to pay attention to your body movements. The ability to analyze people can be invaluable in almost any setting.

How to Analyze People

Though it may sound intimidating, learning to analyze other people is not nearly as difficult as it may initially seem. There are no complicated rules that you need to memorize or any skills that you need to learn—all you have to do is learn the pattern of behaviors and what they mean. This is because once you know the behaviors; you can usually start to piece together the intent behind the behaviors.

You can begin to find out exactly what it is that someone's eyes narrowing means and then begin to identify it with the context of several other actions or behaviors as well. You can find out what is intended when someone's speech and their body language do not match up. Body language rarely lies when people are unaware of how it works, so you can often turn to it for crucial information if you are interacting with other people.

The reason this works to understand people is because it is commonly accepted that there is a cycle between thoughts, feelings, and behaviors. Your thoughts create feelings, and the feelings you have automatically influence your behaviors, as you can see through body language.

Effectively, you will be looking at behaviors that people display and then tracing them back to the feelings behind them. This is why body language is so important to understand. When you can understand what is going on with someone's behavior, you can understand their feelings. When you understand their feelings, you can begin to find out the underlying thoughts that they have. This is about the closest thing to mind reading that you can ever truly attain.

To analyze other people, you have a simple process to get through—you must first find out the neutral baseline of behavior. This is the default behavior of the person. You must then begin to look for deviations in that neutral behavior. From there, you try to put together clusters of behaviors to find out what is going on in the mid of someone else, and then you analyze. This process is not difficult, and if you can learn how to do so, while also learning how to interpret the various types of body language, you will find that understanding other people could never be easier.

When to Analyze People

Analyzing people is one of those skills that can be used in almost any context. You can use it at work, in personal relationships, in politics, religion, and even just in day-to-day life. Because of this versatility, you may find that you are constantly analyzing people, and that is okay. Remember, your unconscious mind already makes snapshot judgments about other people and their intentions, so you were already analyzing people, to begin with. Now, you are simply making an effort to ensure that those analyses are made in your conscious mind so you can be aware of them.

Now, let's take a look at several different compelling situations in which being able to consciously analyze someone is a critical skill to know:

In parenting: When you can analyze other people, you can begin to use those skills toward your children. Now, you may be thinking that a child's mind is not sophisticated enough to get a reliable read on, but remember, the child's feelings are usually entirely genuine. In essence, they have their feelings that they have, and though the reason behind those feelings may be less than compelling to you as a parent, that does not in any way dismiss the feelings. By being able to recognize the child's emotions, you can begin to understand what is going on in your child's mind, and that will allow you to parent calmly and more effectively.

In relationships: When you live with someone else, it can be incredibly easy to step on someone else's toes without realizing it. Of course, constantly stepping on the toes of someone else is likely to lead to some degree of resentment if it is never addressed.

Yet, some people have a hard time discussing when they are uncomfortable or miserable. This is where being able to analyze someone else comes in—you will be able to tell what your partner's base emotions are when you interact, allowing you to play the role of support.

In the workplace: Especially if you interact with other people, you need to be able to analyze other people. You will be able to see how your coworkers view you, allowing you to change your behaviors to get the company image that you desire. Beyond just that, you may also work in a field that requires you to be able to get good reads on someone in the first place.

In public: When you are interacting with people in public, you need to be able to protect yourself. When you can read other people, you can find out whether you are safe or whether someone is threatening or suspicious. This means that you can prepare yourself no matter what the situation is to ensure that you are always ready to respond.

In an interview, you may find that read an interviewer's body language can give you a clue on when to change tactics or move on to something else. You will be able to tell how you are being taken simply by watching for body language and other nonverbal cues.

In other words, you deem the person speaking authority and therefore deem them to be trustworthy. Instead, make an effort to see the other party as what they truly are by learning to read their body language. You can tell if the politician on television is uncomfortable or lying simply by learning to analyze their behaviors.

In arguments: When you are arguing with someone else, usually, emotions are running high on both ends. No one is thinking clearly, and things that were not meant can be said. However, when you can analyze people, you can start to find out when someone else is getting emotional to disengage altogether.

In self-reflection: When you can analyze other people, you can start to analyze yourself as well. This means that you can stop and look at your body language to sort of check-in with yourself and find out what is going on in your mind. Sometimes, it can be difficult to identify exactly how you are feeling, but this is the perfect way to do so in a pinch. If you can stop and self-reflect, you can identify your emotions.

In self-regulation: Identifying your emotions then lends itself to the ability to self-regulate. When you are, for example, in a heated argument and feel yourself tensing up and getting annoyed, you may be able to key into the fact that you are getting annoyed and respond accordingly. Conversely, when you can analyze other people, you can look at them and see how they are feeling. This means that if you can see that you are intimidating or making someone uncomfortable, you can make the necessary changes to your actions.

Chapter 12 Mind Control

Mind control sounds like a devious plot in a movie, but you have most likely experienced it many times a day for many years and never noticed it. Mind control, or the idea of thought-reform, is a controversial theory and practice, but one that does not necessarily mean tricking and scheming. As a matter of fact, mind control can be as simple as subliminal suggestion used to steer one in the direction you want rather than the direction they were going autonomously.

Every day, you are exposed to one form of mind control or another, product placement on television and in movies. The music you hear in a store or even an elevator. Friends that are so convincing, you can't help but agree, or you find yourself always saying yes to them.

While on the topic of your goals and what you want to achieve, it is imperative to stress the importance of what you want to achieve. If others are consistently being spoken with on how important the idea or goal is, and specifics on why it is so important, eventually they start to see your idea as more than just something you want, but an issue of utmost importance. Your thought or goal becomes something more and it should be more to you too. It should be a movement. A goal doesn't have to be a social ideal to be a movement; you just need others to feel its importance as much as you do.

So, your idea, goal, or thought is now more than just something you want. Other people want it too. And it is not just important, it is imperative. And it needs to happen now. Creating a sense of urgency is another effective form of utilizing mind control techniques to your benefit. Making urgent statements, or claiming that this situation is time sensitive will create an emotional response in those you wish to influence or persuade. A specific deadline needs to be in place, but the idea that this can't wait long needs to be an underlying sentiment

Being consistent is the core aspect of implementing mind control techniques to get what you want. Consistently repeating what you want, and be consistent when rejecting old ideas or goals. Be consistent when speaking about what needs to happen, when and why. These factors should be underlined, in bold print, repeated regularly, and the time sensitivity need to be stressed.

There is nothing wrong with being a little pushy to get what you want out of your life. Another great technique when using mind control is to ask small things of others, or asking for small changes in another's ideas, and then expanding from there. Let's use a raise from your employer as an example. If you want a decent increase in pay, don't ask for your top dollar pay increase. Ask for a small increase in pay based on your performance and loyalty. Your boss will agree (considering you are worthy of the raise to begin with) and think that they got off cheap keeping you happy. After you have reached the first step in reaching your ultimate pay goal, ask for more work. Let your employer know you are more than happy taking on more responsibility. You can possibly save them money if you are doing more work than before, they may not have to hire another employee to work weekends if you are willing to come in for a few hours on a Saturday. Now, you have a pay increase, but you have more responsibility. It only seems fair that you are paid a little more now that you are a more valuable resource for your employer to utilize. It's better they give you another slight pay increase to cover your knowledge and expertise in the workplace than bother trying to hire another employee to replace you. You see how simple it can be? Now, that isn't saying that you have a boss or employer this would work on, but if you are implementing the other tools you have in your fast-growing arsenal, you are now a very well-liked employee and co-worker who knows how to influence and persuade others to see things the way you do. Your employer may dislike the idea of paying you even more than before, but sometimes it's not just your work ethic that matters, sometimes it's what you bring to the table for everyone you encounter.

It is not easy to say no to someone who you feel a debt to. The final technique of mood control we should consider is generosity. You should always strive to give more than you take from others. When you give more of your time, your effort, your attention, to others, they appreciate it. They remember it. And, when the moment comes that you want something in return, it is much harder to say no, or disagree, or refuse to cooperate with another who has freely offered up so much to them. Even in circumstances or changes others may not want to agree or get on board with, if they know that you have been offered the same courtesy by you previously, they find it hard to go against you. It falls back to persuasion, influence, and reciprocation. Most often, those that you have committed your time and attention to will return the favor, even if you are met with resistance by someone who you have given to, a gentle reminder of what you have done for them is often all that is needed to get them on board with what you want. Sometimes it isn't the loudest voice in the room that matters, but the most consistent and softest from the individual who has done the most to help others. That soft but firm voice can be yours; you only need to take your opportunities as they present themselves.

Who uses mind control?

Media Producers

Just as our five senses are our guides in life, they can also be our enemies and traitors. Our sense of sight and the visual processing areas of the brain are very powerful. We almost always dream visually, even if another sense is missing, and we usually picture someone we are remembering rather than associating some other sensory input with them. This makes imagery and visual manipulation a particularly powerful technique of media mind control.

Traditionally, media production was in the hands of companies and institutions. These manipulative entities were able to pioneer the use of visual, subliminal mind control. Examples include split-second pictures of a product or person inserted into a seemingly innocent movie, such split-second images, which the person perceives as nothing more than a flash of light, are able to take powerful control of a person's emotions.

Sound is another way in which a person is vulnerable to undetected mind control. Both experiments and personal experience will confirm this to you. Have you ever loved a song until it stuck in your head? How easy was it to get rid of? The sound had a powerful influence over you, even though you knew it was present. The power of audio manipulation is even greater when it is undetected.

Lovers

People are always a product of the environment they are in, whether they want to be or not. The way people are raised directly affects the way they act in later life. Someone who is raised by alcoholics has a greater chance of becoming alcoholics in adult life, or they may choose never to drink at all. People who are raised in a house where everything is forbidden may cut loose and go a bit crazy when they are finally out on their own. People who are raised in total disorganization may grow up to be totally obsessive about household cleanliness.

Nurture affects people in other, less severe ways, too. Many people believe that Mom's meatloaf is the absolute best and no other recipe exists. People come from different religious and economic backgrounds. People have different beliefs about what is good and bad, what is acceptable and unacceptable. The problem comes when two people are trying to have a relationship, but neither wants to change their way of thinking. When that happens there is no relationship. There are just two people living together under the same roof.

Sales people

If a salesperson asks a regular customer to write a brief endorsement of the product they buy, hopefully, they will say yes. If someone asks their significant other to take some of the business cards to pass out at work, hopefully, they will say yes. If you write any kind of blog and ask another blogger to provide a link to yours on their blog, hopefully, they will say yes. When enough people say yes, the business or blog will begin to grow. With even more yesses, it will continue to grow and thrive. This is the very simple basis of marketing. Marketing is nothing more than using mind control to get other people to buy something or to do something beneficial for someone else. And the techniques can easily be learned.

Writers

Think of writing a guest spot for someone else who has their own blog. By sending in the entire manuscript first, there is a greater risk of rejection. Begin small. Send them a paragraph or two discussing them the idea. Then make an outline of the idea and send that in an email. Then write the complete draft you would like them too use and send it along. When asking a customer for a testimonial, start by asking for a few lines in an email. Then ask the customer to expand those few lines into a testimonial that covers at least half a typed page. Soon the customer will be ready for an hour-long webcast extolling the virtues of the product and your great customer service skills.

Everything must have a deadline that really exists. The important word here is the word 'real'. That is a total fabrication and everyone knows it to be true. There are no impending other customers and the deal is not going to disappear. There is no real sense of urgency involved. But everyone does it. There are too many situations where people are given a totally fake deadline by someone who thinks it will instill a great sense of urgency for completion of the task. It is not only totally not effective but completely unneeded. It is a simple matter to create true urgency.

In Education

By educating impressionable children, society essentially teaches them to become "ideal" members of society. They are taught and trained in certain ways that fulfil the desires of the government and authorities, and most people don't even think twice about it.

Advertising and Propaganda

By putting advertising and propaganda everywhere, those in control are capable of eliminating people's feeling of self-worth and encourage them to need what is being sold, as opposed to just wanting it. This is essentially a subliminal strategy to make people feel poorly about themselves so that they will purchase whatever is being advertised to increase their feelings of self-worth.

Sports, Politics, Religion

The idea of these strategies is to "divide and conquer". Ultimately, each one has people placed into various categories, where they feel very strongly. As a result, they don't come together and support one another, but rather they are against each other. This means that they are divided, and so the authority can conquer.

Chapter 13 Mind Control Techniques

Persuasion technique is another manipulation technique of the human mind, whereby the manipulated party is aware of what caused his/her opinion shift. The main basis of persuasion is to try and access an individual's right brain. The left half of the brain tends to be rational and analytical. The right half is imaginative and creative.

The idea of persuasion is to distract one's left brain side and keep it busy. Basically, the persuader will generate an eye-opening modified state of consciousness, in turn causing the shift from Beta state awareness, into Alpha in a victim.

This type of activity carried out by the brain of a shift can be measured using an EEG machine. Politicians normally use these techniques in daily lives, in gatherings or during campaigns, lawyers also use it in many variations and are known as tightening the noose.

During a politician's speech, the politician might generate what is known as a yes set. The yes set are basically statements that are made by the politician which will cause the listeners to agree. The listeners might even nod their heads unknowingly in agreement. This act is followed by the truisms. Truisms are basically facts which could be debated, however, once a politician has the target audience agreeing, then the odds are always in the favor of politicians since the audience will stop to think for themselves, thereby continuing to be in agreement. Lastly is the suggestion. The suggestions will entail what the politician will want you to execute or do and since you have been in agreement all along, then you could be easily persuaded to agree with the suggestions.

The techniques and concepts of Neuro-Linguistics are heavily protected. The neuro-Linguistic training is available to individuals who are willing to devote their time and money to the program. The persuasion technique contains some of the most subtle and powerful manipulations. It also entails a manipulation tactic called an intersperse technique and the idea behind this technique is to mention one thing with words but at the same time plant a subliminal impression of another thing in the minds of viewers and listeners.

Vibrato

Vibrato refers to the tremulous effect that's imparted in numerous instrumental and vocal music, using a cycle-per-second range which causes people to go in an altered state of awareness.

At a given point in English history, all singers whose voices included pronounced vibrato could not perform publicly because the listeners would end up having fantasies and going into an altered state, often sensual in nature. People who attend opera or enjoy familiar music to it are affected by an altered state that's induced by performers.

Isolation

This technique entails inducing the loss of reality through the physical separation from friends, family, rational references and society. Isolation of physical nature tends to be extremely powerful, however even in instances physical isolation is not practical or impossible, the manipulators will attempt to segregate you mentally.

This can be achieved in several ways from going for two weeks of seminars in another country to condemning your family members, friends, and colleagues. Limiting any form of influence by controlling the information flow is normally the ultimate goal.

Advertising and Propaganda

This mind-controlling technique involves the use of mass media. These media forms are designed to reach as many people as they can. Mass media include movies, television, radio, magazines, daily newspapers, video games, records, and the internet.

Quite a number of researches have been carried out in the past decades to try and measure the effects of the mass media on the general population. These were done in order to come up with the best techniques to try and influence it. From this research, the field of science of Communications was developed, which is used in public relations, marketing, and politics. Mass communication is an important tool to protect the functionality of democracy.

Edward Bernays is cited as the founder of the consumerist culture, which was designed to target people's self-image primarily in order to turn them went into a need. Initially, this was envisioned for certain products like cigarettes. However, Bernays also pointed out in his 1928 book, Propaganda, that "propaganda" happens to be the executive arm of the useable government." We can see this most clearly in the current police state and the ever-growing snitch culture, wrapped up with the pseudo-patriotic fight on Terror. The ever-increasing consolidation of media has authorized the whole existing corporate structure to consolidate with the government that now utilizes the ideology of propaganda placement. Media; television, print, cable news and movie can now seamlessly work to merge an overall message that may seem to have a ring of truth mainly because they come from a number of sources. When one eventually becomes accustomed to identifying the main "message," one will be able to see this type of imprinting everywhere, notwithstanding the subliminal messaging.

Ways of Controlling the Mind

The mind can be taught not to be controlled by others. There are various ways people in society can achieve this.

Believe in yourself and what you can change.

Someone who wants to be strong in mind needs to believe. If a victim doesn't believe that they can change, then they are not going to try as hard as they can if they believe success is a possibility. Thus, making sure that they are using positive thinking to face their problems. Keeping in mind that they can change the way they think hence they can improve. Different studies that have been conducted have shown that people who adopt a "growth" mindset tend to be more likely to make coveted improvements compared to those who view their skills and traits as unchangeable and fixed.

Be optimistic with your abilities

Many people tend to think that being accurate about their abilities to control themselves is key. Nonetheless, studies show that by being more optimistic with your ability to take full control of your behavior then you will be able to achieve more self-control.

To become optimistic, try and tell your inner self that you are going to succeed and gain full control of your mind, over and over, irrespective as to whether you believe it or not.

Also, try to remind yourself of the times where you managed to successfully control your brain and mind as intended. You should reflect on the successes and not on any form of self-control failures that you may have had.

Stop overgeneralizing

Overgeneralizing simply refers to the process of taking one occurrence of a negative experience and then projecting the experience onto other experiences or alternatively to your predictions about how your future is going to be. People need to use this opportunity to transform their own future through constant persistence and by working hard. For instance, someone who had a strenuous childhood and thinks that their life is going to be challenging forever, need to might ways in which he wants his life to improve, and work to improve them. Those who may want a more meaningful relationship or a better job may have to research on the different ways of attaining these things. The individual should then set goals for oneself in the different domains to accomplish.

Stop jumping to conclusions

This tactic is a thought trap that entails thinking certain things without having any sort of evidence to back the thoughts up. A person who tends to jump to conclusions may think that a person despises him or her without having any evidence that supports this assertion. For one to jump into conclusions, then they can employ different ways including pausing and thinking more, before reaching any judgments. It can help to ask yourself questions about the thought. And individual can ask himself if he really knows that the thought, he is having is true or false. He can also ask himself to identify detailed pieces of evidence that would suggest that the thought is true. Someone who believes a person doesn't like him/he may have to ask themselves to identify specific conversations with the individual to offer evidence for their claims.

Avoid catastrophizing

The act of catastrophizing is simply defined as a pessimistic thought trap whereby the person tends to exaggerate scenarios or situations. A person who is catastrophizing after failing an examination may utter statements like "My life is ruined. I am never going to get a great job. To prevent yourself from catastrophizing, the person needs to work on processing things in a positive manner. He can also ask oneself questions that employ reason and logic. People who have just failed a test and believe that their life is ruined because they are never going to get a great job may ask oneself: "Do I know anyone who has failed a test yet still gotten a good job and/or seems happy?" "If I was hiring someone would I make my entire decision based on that person's grade in a single class?"

Create obstacles for yourself

The best way to control the mind is by making it more difficult for the mind to get what it needs. You should starve it sometimes. The added effort will enable this part of the mind, which is less likely to win and influence one's behavior. Instances when one keeps clicking on the snooze button early in the morning, he could place the phone far from the bed. This will force the individual to get out of their beds so as to turn it off. Another model is when you want to control the part of the mind which wants to watch TV when a part of you is keen on cutting down on the TV watching time, you could put your remote control in a difficult to reach the spot.

Reward your successful self-control efforts

This technique is really helpful as a kind of motivation. A great example, if you do not feel like doing laundry and cleaning the house but you managed to force yourself to do the test anyway, then you should reward yourself with your favorite pastime activity. However, be careful not to make the reward/gift too excessive or you might find yourself beyond control and then back to where you started from. If your main goal is to be able to study and you managed to force the mind and managed to do the studying when you actually never felt like doing, then do not treat yourself too much or you might just end up losing the progress that you have made.

Punish the unsuccessful self-control efforts

While we rewarding good behavior and success, it's also important to punish yourself for any failures on self-control. As a matter of fact, studies indicate that the threat of punishment forces the mind to embrace self-control.

To ascertain that the punishment was effective, ensure that you place the punishment on another person's mind either a close friend, partner or family member.

A great example is that you could ask them to ask your dessert. If at the end of the day you failed to gain the established self-control measures, then they are going to withhold the dessert.

Chapter 14 Assuming Success

Success and failure are both normal parts of life.

Assuming success means making good choices that will point toward success. Spend time on those things that matter and leave the unimportant things behind. The focus should always be on the big picture and never on moments where gratification is instant. Assuming success will also mean being ready to accept the responsibility for success and being accountable to use it correctly. It involves doing what is right and not just taking the easiest path to completion. Always be prepared to follow the path to the decided goal.

Each day is full of decisions that might affect the future of life as it is known now. Every day people must choose what to do and what things to say. Choices must be made to either be well behaved or to misbehave. Every day of every life is potentially filled with choices to be made that might actually affect the very outcome of life in the future. The burning question is whether the choices made today will lead toward future success. The answer should be a completely honest one because it is vital to the success of future decisions.

Making good choices is never easy. Good choices are difficult ones. But it is the good choices that will eventually lead to success. The first good choices are the hardest ones, especially if making good choices has not been a regular habit in the past. But each subsequent good choice will cause making good choices to become easier.

Some people will spend the whole of their lives trying to figure out how to be successful. Personal success is an achievable goal for anyone who truly wants to achieve success. Most people do want to be independent financially, to enjoy a wonderful career, and to have a strong and satisfying home life. People want to know they are important, that they matter to someone else, at least one someone else. Almost everyone wants to do at least one wonderful thing in their life. This is how most people measure the extent of success.

And achieving success is not dependent on built-in ability, intelligence, or background. Success does not care who a person knows. Everyone has the ability to do wonderful things in life and to achieve success. The key is to assume that success is the ultimate goal and no other potential outcome will be acceptable.

Do not be afraid to question the path of life if it is not leading toward success. It is quite alright to ask questions of other people if it is necessary to learn how to reach success. Just never assume that someone else's path will be the only one that exists. Everyone must choose a personal path to success. Everyone must define the idea of success for themselves. Take in advice from others and use the tips and tricks that make sense. Discard the rest. Only do what feels tight and acceptable.

The first goal achieved is perhaps the most important goal on the road to success. The first goal proves that goals can be achieved. The first goal will begin to program the brain to accept the idea of success and to develop new pathways that will facilitate becoming successful. People will only learn to succeed by achieving success. The more goals that are achieved, the more goals people want to achieve. Success builds confidence that leads to more goal achievement that leads to more success that leads to more confidence. It grows in an ever-widening circle.

The only real limit on success is a personal limit. With the true success, the sky is the limit. Once the decision to push aside limits of the mind has been made, then anything can be achieved. If goal accomplishment is approached with a completely open heart and mind then anything can be achieved. Once the habit of achieving goals is begun, there really is no limit on personal success. As long as progress is not halted, then success is practically guaranteed.

Be prepared to chase success mercilessly. Success is a goal and a way of life. Once success is first achieved, it creates a burning desire for more success. Never be content to stop with just one success. Always strive for more success.

Realize that sometimes life flows a certain direction and that direction cannot be changed. There are times that life will get in the way of the pursuit of success. Recognize these moments for temporary distractions and not permanent set-in-stone ways of life. All life choices will go off the rails at times. The path to achieving a goal can be disrupted by unexpected roadblocks. Life happens. Never lose sight of success or allow these interruptions to permanently derail the success train.

Always try to set goals that are realistic and achievable. No one can possibly hope to lose one hundred pounds overnight, or even in one month. That is not a realistic goal. Instead, be prepared to set many small goals that will lead to the achievement of the ultimate goal. There is no miracle transformation in sight. But, through hard work and attention to detail goal will be achieved and success will be assured.

Remember to stay positive. Positive feelings will enable the mind to create greater thought patterns that will lead to the brain making more connections between thoughts and ideas. Connections that are new and fresh to the mind can easily lead to a rush of creative thoughts. These creative thoughts can easily ferment in the mind and lead to wonderful new thoughts in the future. Learn to relax. Anger and stress are definite creativity killers. Using relaxation techniques will recharge the brain and relax the nerves to allow positive thoughts to flow through more freely. Before pondering any problem, take a few minutes to breathe deeply and relax.

Do not make the mistake of being too nice when traveling the path to success. Of course, everyone wants to treat themselves nicely, even if it is only occasionally, but do not make the mistake of being too nice to the mind. Pamper the body and work the mind. Of course, making extremely negative personal comments is never a good idea. The comments like "You are so fat" and "You will never amount to anything" are definitely self-defeating. But do not be too easy on that person inside who craves success. Being too nice can have negative consequences. Being too nice usually means not pushing oneself to one's ultimate potential. Failure is okay because it is expected. Thoughts like these will never lead to ultimate success. It is okay to be a little tough every now and then. No great goal was ever reached without a lot of sweat and agony. Be prepared to suffer. Suffering now just makes success all that much sweeter when it does arrive.

Success begins with a dream. Anything worth having is worth dreaming about. Open the heart and the mind to the possibility of success. Take the time to wonder how life will change when success is achieved. Think only positive thoughts. Negative thoughts are too discouraging. Dream of all the possibilities that come with real success. Keep the dream alive, fan its flames every time it seems to be growing cold. Never let the dream go away.

The dream of success needs to be big, huge, enormous. The dream of success needs to feel much bigger than anything that might be achieved in this life. In addition to feeling really intense, it also needs to be something that is believable. The dream must be seen as something that it is possible to achieve if everything falls into place correctly. If hard work if offered, if other people lend a hand, if certain life events happen at the right time, then the dream of success is one that can be achieved.

Everyone who is able to achieve great things is able to see those great things in their minds. They can picture themselves wallowing in success, whatever success means to them. Imagining a successful outcome makes achieving a successful outcome much more realistic. A basketball player will imagine the ball going through the net with every shot. A pageant queen will imagine the crown on her head. A jockey will imagine his horse crossing the finish line first. Imagining something to be a reality is the first step into making it a reality. And creating reality is the first step toward assuming success and all the perks that come with it.

Success depends greatly on mind control and assuming success is just another way to practice mind control to create a goal of success. Success itself is both a goal and a way of life. It is possible to program the mind to focus more completely on the idea of achieving success. Remember that every habit and every thought, both positive and negative, has its own pathway in the mind. All these pathways are created through repeated practice of these habits and thoughts. Negative thoughts will need to be replaced by positive thoughts. Negative habits will need to be replaced by positive habits. All negativity will create roadblocks to true success. The pathways of negative thoughts and habits will be eliminated by the practice of positive thoughts and habits. Success is one of these positive habits.

Chapter 15 How to use Dark Psychology in Your Daily Life

How Psychology Can Improve Your Life?

The following are some of the top ten realistic uses for psychology in regular life:

1. Get Prompted

Whether your purpose is to stop smoking, lose weight, or examine a new language, some training from psychology provides pointers for buying motivated. To grow your motivation while drawing close a project, make use of some of the subsequent tips derived from research in cognitive and educational psychology:

Introduce new or novel factors to hold your interest high.

Vary the series to help stave off boredom.

Study new matters that build on your present understanding.

Set clear goals that might be at once related to the assignment.

2. Enhance Your Management Abilities

It doesn't count number in case you're an office supervisor or a volunteer at a neighborhood teenage activity group, having true leadership abilities will in all likelihood, be vital sometime in the future for your existence. Now, not all of us is a born leader, but some easy suggestions taken from mental studies can help you improve your leadership capabilities.

One of the most famous research papers on this topic looked at three distinct management styles. Primarily based on the findings of this look at and subsequent studies, practice several the following when you are in a management function:

Offer clear steering but permit group contributors to voice opinions.

Communicate approximately possible answers to troubles with contributors to the group.

Focus on stimulating ideas and be inclined to praise creativity.

3. Come To Be A Better Communicator

Conversation involves a whole lot more than just the way you speak or write. Research indicates that nonverbal indicators make up a big portion of our interpersonal communications

Some key strategies encompass the subsequent:

Use proper eye contact.

Start noticing nonverbal indicators in others.

Learn to use your tone of voice to boost your message.

4. Learn To Better Understand Others

Just like nonverbal communication, your capacity to apprehend your emotions and the feelings of those around you perform an important role in your relationships and professional lifestyles. The time emotional intelligence refers to your potential to apprehend each of your emotions in addition to those of other human beings.

What can you do to emerge as more emotionally stable? Recall a few the subsequent techniques:

Cautiously assess your very own emotional reactions.

Record your enjoyment and emotions in a journal.

Try to see situations from the angle of a different person.

5. Make Extra Correct Selections

Studies in cognitive psychology supply a wealth of statistics about choice making. By making use of those techniques for your lifestyles, you can discover ways to make wiser choices. The following time you want to make a huge decision, strive the usage of several the subsequent techniques:

Try using the "Six Thinking Hats" technique with the aid of searching on the situation from multiple points of view, including rational, emotional, intuitive, creative, advantageous, and Dark views.

Recall the capacity prices and blessings of choice.

Appoint a grid evaluation approach that offers a score for how a selected decision will fulfill unique requirements you may have.

6. Enhance Your Reminiscence

Have you ever wondered why you can remember the precise information of childhood events yet forget the call of the new customer you met yesterday? Research on how we form new reminiscences as well as how and why we forget has caused some of the findings that can be implemented without delay in your daily life.

What are some methods you can grow your reminiscence of electricity?

Awareness of the data.

Rehearse what you have discovered.

Do away with distractions.

7. Make Wiser financial decisions

Nobel Prize-winning psychologist Daniel Kahneman and his colleague Amos Tversky performed a chain of research that looked at how humans manipulate uncertainty and danger while making decisions.

One looks at located that workers could extra than triple their financial savings by making use of some of the following strategies:

Don't procrastinate. Start investing savings now.

Commit earlier to dedicate quantities of your future profits in your retirement financial savings.

Try to be aware of non-public biases that may result in Dark money choices.

8. Get Higher Grades

The subsequent time you are tempted to whine about pop quizzes, midterms, or finals, consider that research has confirmed that taking checks honestly helps you better consider what you have learned, even if it wasn't on the test.

Every other study discovered that repeated check-taking might be a higher reminiscence aid than studying. College students who were tested again and again have been able to remember 61% of the content while the ones within the have a look at group recalled most effective 40%. How can you observe those findings to your lifestyles? While seeking to research new data, self-check frequently to cement what you have learnt, into your memory.

9. Become More Effective

Occasionally, it looks as if there are hundreds of books, blogs, and magazine articles telling us the way to get more completed in an afternoon. However, how much of this advice is based on real studies? As an example, think about the variety of times have you ever heard that multitasking can help you become more productive. Studies have discovered that trying to carry out multiple missions at the same time severely impairs pace, accuracy, and productiveness.

What classes from psychology can you operate to boom your productivity? Consider several the following:

Avoid multitasking while running on complex or dangerous obligations.

Cognizance at the venture at hand.

Eliminate distractions.

10. Be Healthier

Psychology also can be a useful device for improving your ordinary health. From approaches to encourage workout and better nutrients to new remedies for melancholy, the sector of fitness psychology gives a wealth of beneficial strategies that can help you to be more healthy and happier.

Some examples that you may practice at once in your very own existence:

Research has shown that both daylight and synthetic mild can reduce the symptoms of seasonal affective sickness.

Studies have demonstrated that exercise can contribute to more mental well-being.

Studies have determined that supporting people apprehend the dangers of bad behaviors can lead to healthier choices.

Conclusion

People are never as simple as their surfaces. There is always more going on underneath. Should you be troubled by this? If you've lived your life buying the smiling faces and seemingly straightforward motives of your friends and associates, should this hidden reservoir of dark psychology cause you consternation. I don't think so. By letting people be complicated, we're validating them as people. We're letting them exist in our estimations at a higher level than the cardboard cutouts we imagined. There's something a little condescending about imagining a human being as being one-dimensional, a background character in our own lives. No – everyone is the hero of their own story, and everyone is complicated. We do them a great service be recognizing this, and in acknowledging it we take the first step towards living in a more complex, more adult, and ultimately more fulfilling world.

We have talked about the difference between persuasion and manipulation. Both are methods of convincing, of making an argument. The difference, however, is that while the persuader plays fair, winning and argument with logic and appeals, the manipulator acts dishonestly and without the best interests of their audience in mind. Manipulation is something anyone is capable of, but can be easier, and in fact pathological, for those with certain deviant personality types. These include narcissists, whose self-centered worldview overpowers everything else, sociopaths, who lack the ability to feel empathy, and psychotics, who live in worlds of delusion. Manipulators can be dangerous to the well-being of others, and relationships with them can be toxic and difficult to escape. We've also talked about the specific techniques employed by manipulators, with an extended case study into the methods used by cold readers and other purveyors of false psychic phenomena.

The biggest mistake people make is to assume that other people are simple. That they are one note. As we've seen, people put on masks. It's natural. You do it and I do as well. You want to decide what you reveal to the world and what you withhold. But remember, if you're doing it, so is everyone else. Look around you. Some people are smiling, some might have neutral expressions. Maybe you see someone who seems noticeably mad. Each of these people has pain. Deep pain. Maybe it is carried over from childhood. Maybe is finds it source in the disappointments of adulthood, in the fact that reality never lives up to the expectations we start with. Maybe they bury it. Maybe they share it with a therapist. Maybe they've dealt with it and moved on. Or maybe it has taken them over, driven them to drugs or alcohol, or given them issues with mental illness, or made it difficult to form strong relationships. Maybe they cry themselves to sleep every night. But everyone has a dark side.

How can you exist in this world of masks, where you never can know for sure what lurks behind them? A friendly coworker could be a secret manipulator? A potential romantic interest could be an incompatible mess of complex unprocessed trauma. You never know.

The most important first step, which we talked about at some length, is protecting yourself. One way to do this is to deal with your own dark impulses. Don't bottle it up. Don't blame yourself. Don't deny it. Deal with it. Admitting that you are complex, and accepting that this is simply part of being human, will allow you to exist as a more fully integrated and holistically functioning human being. The happiest people are not those who have dealt with the least hardship. They are those who have deal with hardship the best. The other important way to protect you is to be aware of the masks of others. No, you don't have to live in fear of the monster hiding behind the smiling face, but it is important to do your due diligence. Don't assume that the surface is the whole story. It never is. Absolutely never, especially when dealing with new people, be smart and remain observant. And once you feel that you have gathered enough information to understand that this person can, in fact, be trusted, and you begin to let your guard down, don't throw it all away be hiding behind masks of your own. True trust, true love, truly functional relationships, are those in which we can be honest with each other. When we can let each other see behind our masks to the fully realize people that live behind them.

Life is a struggle. Don't expect to get it all right. Don't expect to ever perfect your life, relationships, or personality. The best we can do it to keep diligently trying, cautiously, confidently, optimistically, with open eyes and open hearts.

BODY LANGUAGE AND DARK PSYCHOLOGY:

THE COMPLETE GUIDE TO SPEED-
READING, ANALYZE PEOPLE AND
MASTER THE SECRETS OF HUMAN
BEHAVIOR WITH MANIPULATION AND
MIND CONTROL

Navarro Goleman & Joe Poumpouras

Introduction

What Is Body Language?

Body language is a notion, which men and women that are effective often know well. The analysis and concept of it are become popular lately years since we can comprehend exactly what we 'state' during our bodily gestures and facial expressions, to interpret and show our inherent feelings and perspectives. Body language can also be known as 'non-verbal communications', and much less generally 'on-vocal communications. The term 'same-sex' will be utilized at a wider awareness, and each of these conditions is somewhat obscure. For this guide, the terms 'body language' and 'non-verbal communications' are widely interchangeable. This manual also has the view it is the analysis of how people communicate facial besides the spoken words, and in this regard, the treatment of this topic here is wider than normal guides, that are restricted only to human gestures and positions. If you execute any serious analysis or debate, you should explain the language on your way.

As an instance:

Body language that is does comprise attention and facial expression movement. – Normally, what about perspiration and breathing? - This is dependent upon the definition used. And while pitch and tone of voice signs; is such part of body language? Not normally, but so if considering bodily gestures/expressions and just the phrases, because they could ignore by you. There are no replies to those questions. It is an issue of interpretation. For broadening our range, a reason is to avoid missing important signals which may not be contemplated inside a narrower definition. Nevertheless, confusion arises if definitions and context aren't correctly created, for instance: It's carelessly and commonly quoted that 'on-verbal communications' or 'body language' accounts for as many as 93 percent of their significance that individuals take from any individual communication. This is a simulation-based on the study concept, which while it is something of a basis of body language study didn't create such a claim of Albert Mehrabian. Mehrabian's research findings centered on communications with a strong psychological or 'feelings' component besides, the 93% non-verbal percentage included vocal intonation (paralinguistic), which can be considered by most as falling out the definition. When saying specific care must be resolved figures concerning proportions of conveyed, or in making any company claims concerning communications and body language. It's safe to state that body language signifies a very large percentage of meaning that is conveyed and translated between individuals. Resources and body language specialists appear to agree that between 50-80percent of communications are non-invasive. So, while the data change based on the circumstance, it's usually accepted that non-invasive communications are extremely important in the way we know each other (or fail to), particularly in face-to-face and one-way communications, and most certainly when the communications demand a psychological or sociological element. When we meet somebody for body language is particularly crucial the very first moment. We create and this evaluation relies far more on what we believe in and see about another person that they speak. We produce an opinion about an individual that is brand new before they speak a word. This is quite powerful in forming impressions on meeting somebody. The result occurs both ways - from when we meet with somebody for the very first-time language, the unconscious and conscious levels determine our perception of them.

When someone meets with us, they form their impression from our signs most of us. And this influence continues throughout communications and relationships between individuals. Body language translated and is continually being exchanged on a subconscious level this is occurring Involving individuals of this time. Remember - while you're interpreting (consciously or unconsciously) yours is being continuously interpreted by the body language of individuals, so men and women. The individuals and, with the awareness of abilities body language often get an edge over those whose admiration is restricted to the subconscious.

You may change your consciousness from the unconscious mindful by studying the topic, and then by practicing, you're studying communications on your dealings with other people.

Chapter 1 What is Non-verbal Communication

Have you heard of the phrase "it's not what you say it's how you say it"? There is true meaning behind this as, what we say matters, sure, but the non-verbal cues we give are even more important.. It has been said that more than sixty percent of what you say is in your body language not your actual words.

Learning about non-verbal communication can help you in a variety of ways. You will be more perceptive to what people are actually trying to say. You may also pick up on lies or deceit more easily. Figuring out a person's true motivation can become much clearer when you start to pay attention to what their body is saying.

Paralanguage is part of non-verbal communication. It encompasses a couple of different areas that can help you communicate more effectively. The main pieces of it are tone, cadence, and inflection. All of these elements play a key role in what you are actually saying.

The tone of your voice plays a pretty big role in non-verbal communication, as well. It can draw a listener in or make them totally tune out. A voice that is monotone does not have any inflection. Every word comes out with the same tone and volume. The cadence of a monotone speaker tends to be slow and steady throughout their words. This can be very hard to listen too.

When you are talking with someone changing your tone can help to give them clues as to how you are feeling. It allows for better communication as we are able to express our emotions through the tone of our voices. In public speaking, having a great tone will get you everywhere. Voice inflection is just as important, and both play a big role in effective verbal communication.

If you have a flat voice or you notice that people drift off while you are talking you can practice this. Find your favorite book and practice reading it aloud with different inflections and tones. This can help you during regular conversations to get away from the monotone nature of some voices. You will notice that people around you are more engaged and what you say matters more than it did before.

Para communication is only a piece of non-verbal communication. What else do we need to consider when trying being better non-verbal communicators. This is a tough question as there is quite a bit that encompasses non-verbal communication. We can take a bit of time and look at the tip of the iceberg but know that people spend years studying non-verbal communication.

Reading someone's facial expressions is a major tell in non-verbal communication. There are many exercises that teach us what facial expressions are saying. Some of them are very straightforward. If you look at someone that is smiling it, typically, means they are happy or enjoying what they are doing. However, a smile can be deceiving.

Smiling can also be a sign of anxiety. When people want to fit in but don't know how to do that, they will smile to look more approachable and less nervous. Tight lips can give away these smiles. You may also notice that a smile on someone's face simply looks fake. If you feel this way, it likely is. That goes along with going with your gut.

The more you notice about someone's expression the more you can tell about them. Sure, picking out a smile or a frown is easy but what about the smaller harder to see expressions. Our faces have up to ten thousand different movement patterns and believe it or not they all mean something. Learning more about what facial twitches and twists mean can help you pick out the rats among the group.

Kinesics, or body movement, also play a major role in non-verbal communication, the gestures that we make during conversations tell a lot about how we are feeling.

If we are interested in what is being said or we are nervous about it. Paying attention to how people's bodies are moving will tell you volumes about what they are thinking and feeling.

Think about the last meeting you were sitting in, did you see the person nervously drumming their fingers on the table or their thighs? This is a sign of boredom, irritability, and nervousness. This can be very distracting to a group and should be avoided. If you are one to take to these body movements keep in mind that the best thing you can do is keep your hands on the table. Clasping them can help keep you from the annoying drumming that your feelings are pushing you toward.

We are used to the meaning of some body movements. When we are having a conversation and someone is looking at us and nodding as we speak, we know this means they are paying attention and actively listening to what we have today. Some may be nodding but not actually engaged. You can see this through their eye movement. This could be from boredom or preoccupied thinking.

While both of these examples are easy to spot there are a few body movements that aren't as easy to determine meaning from. Someone that frequently clears their throat is likely nervous about what they are saying, however, they may just be trying to get someone's attention that is distracted.

Nervous ticks are commonly seen in people that are going to do something against the law or something harmful to others. Unless you are deep in the traits of the Dark Triad, you likely feel some sort of guilt when doing something wrong. This can lead to body movement clues as your body is rejecting the act that is about to be performed.

Noticing these ticks can give you great insight as to the intentions of a person. It can be a simple twitch of the hand or odd mouth movements. It could even be a jerking of the head or other limbs. So, while bouncing of knees or drumming of fingers are consistent views that somebody is nervous or bored. There are tells when somebody has something worse on their mind.

Another major component in non-verbal communication is eye contact. It can be very difficult for some people to maintain eye contact. This can make you feel as if they are not listening or that they are Shifty. For some, it is neither of these things. They simply find it to be uncomfortable to look somebody in the eyes while talking.

Maintaining a certain level of eye contact with somebody you are talking to shows that you are interested and engaged in what they are saying. This does not mean that you need to stare at them the entire time that they are talking. However, frequent eye contact can truly help improve communication.

Experts have found that when looking somebody in the eye it can be more comfortable when you look at their other features as well. Varying your site to look at their eyelids nose and around the other areas of their face can make it less uncomfortable. Of course, you will also want to take the time to actually look them in the eyes as they are speaking.

People that have committed crimes or that intend on committing crimes have a hard time maintaining contact. It has been said that the eyes are the window to the soul and there is definitely some truth in this. When you notice how somebody's eyes move and look it can help you to determine their intent whether it be good or bad.

When looking at nonverbal communication and people that truly command attention a lot of it is said through their posture. Your posture says a lot about not only you and your confidence levels but also your position in life. When we talked about your posture we're not only speaking of when you're standing up at also plays a role when you are sitting down.

Open and closed posture also play a role in how people perceive you. If you are accepting of people coming up and talking to you, you will want to use an open posture. This looks like a pretty relaxed position. Your shoulders and hips will be equally spread and you won't be standing at attention. You will leave your stomach exposed rather than crossing your arms over top of it. Standing this way makes you more approachable. It will make it so that people trust you more easily and are willing to have conversations with you at any point.

A closed pasture going to have the exact opposite effect, if you were sitting in the chair with your arms crossed over your stomach and your legs crossed, as well, you are telling people to stay away. This type of positioning can make it look like you are very bored. It also tells people that you are unapproachable and unwilling to open up to them. This causes distrust and tends to lead to poor communication.

Proxemics is another important factor in nonverbal communication. This genuinely has to do with people's personal space and their comfort levels. Most people want you to stay outside of their "personal bubble". Most are comfortable standing in conversation with somebody they don't know when that person is a foot or more away from them. Obviously, the people that we care about can be closer to us without making us uncomfortable. This goes for family members, people you are in relationships with, and close friends.

Taking notice to not only other people's personal space but your own is important. Some people that would like to victimize you will try and get in close. They realize that touching somebody makes a connection. They will Honan on their ability to come into close contact with you and then take advantage of it. So making sure that you stand a reasonable distance away from people will stop this behavior from occurring. In addition, if somebody is a bit touchy feely there is nothing wrong with telling them that it makes you uncomfortable. Letting them know that it is not okay to be in your personal space can save you from harm in the future.

In a business atmosphere, you want to make sure that you are not overly far away from someone. If you are very far away during a conversation and it may seem as if you are disinterested. It is easier to get distracted while somebody is talking if you're not near to them. Knowing the appropriate distance four conversations is important for most people. It's really can help you to communicate more effectively.

The last area to look at and nonverbal communication is psychological changes. These can be quite hard to notice but with practice it can become easier. This type of communication is related to our emotions. When we use the word psychological changes, we are talking about noticing if somebody starts to sweat or their face turns red from embarrassment. These are surefire ways to tell that somebody is feeling uncomfortable or uneasy about their current situation.

If you are dealing with a friend that gets teary-eyed while you're talking you probably need to change your tactics to make them feel more comfortable. Putting somebody at ease when they are feeling nervous can truly help to build your rapport with them. Of course, you want to be careful when dealing with people that you don't know very well. They can pick up on your psychological changes and, in turn, use them against you.

Chapter 2 Personality Types

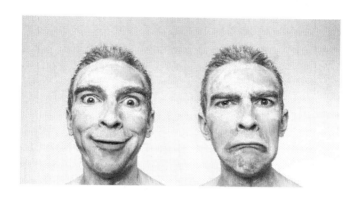

When you interact with a person for a while, you can interpret and tell the type of personality they are. Personality type refers to the different types of individuals as have been classified through psychology based on the way they tend to behave, feel, and think. Personality is what makes a person who they are, and each person has an idea of their personality type. Some people are thick-skinned, others are sensitive, and others are bubbly while others are reserved.

Several ways have been put forward to measure personality, but mostly, psychologists focus on personality traits. The Big Five has come to be the most widely accepted of these traits. It is also called the FFM standing for the five-factor model or the OCEAN.

These five factors are the ones expressed by the acronym CANOE or OCEAN. These factors are affected by how someone was brought up. Genetics and the environment affect these personality traits almost equally. Let us dive in and analyze each of these five broad types of personalities and the attributes associated with each one of them so that you can know to interpret them.

Extraversion

This is the widely recognized personality type. It is common for you to hear people say that someone is either an extrovert or an introvert. This personality type is based on someone having a lot of interaction with the external world. Extraverts are known to be a kind of social butterflies and drive pleasure from interactions with others and are often known to be full of energy. They are lively, sociable, and chatty, and they draw power and energy from their interactions with crowds. They are action-oriented persons and tend to be enthusiastic. They are assertive and talkative and have high group visibility .they may dominance in social settings.

On the other hand, introverts have lower energy and are less involved with the social world. They have lower engagement with the social world and deliberately tend to be low-key and quiet. This should not be confused with being shy or depressed but being more independent of their social world. Being shy refers to the fear of social situations and interactions or being unable to function socially, but an introvert can be charming at parties and come-together events with colleagues. They like to have their time alone and require less social stimulation, not because they are antisocial or unfriendly, but because they are reserved in social events. They just prefer being solo or in small-group activities.

Agreeableness

Individuals with this personality have a general concern for social harmony. People with agreeable personality place premium value in getting along well with others, and they have the willingness to consider other people even if it means sacrificing self-interests. They are associated with kindness, being helpful, generosity, and being trusting and trustworthy. They are optimistic about their look of humanity.

On the other hand, disagreeable individuals put their self-interest first at the expense of good relations with others. They have less concern about other peoples' wellbeing and will rarely reach out for others. They tend not to be friendly or cooperative because they are skeptical and suspicious of others. They are seen as being argumentative, challenging, competitive, or untrustworthy people.

Openness

People with this type of personality are open to the experience. They have a general appreciation for adventure, art, imagination, unusual ideas, emotion, and other experiences. They are open to the excitement, have intellectual curiosity, sensitive to beauty, and are always ready to experiment with new things. They have a good understanding of their feelings and are associated with creativity. Scoring high on openness may be taken to mean that they are hard to predict, can hold unconventional beliefs, may lack focus, and indulge in risky behavior such as taking drugs. Individuals in this category seek to actualize themselves through euphoric and intense experiences.

Conversely, people with low openness are pragmatic and data-driven and seek to gain fulfillment through endurance. They are seen to have closed minds and are perceived to be dogmatic. They are better off sticking to their habits, avoid adventurous activities, and tend not to like new experiences.

Neuroticism

Individuals in this category tend to experience negative emotions. These emotions include depression, anger, or anxiety. It is associated with emotional instability and connected to low tolerance for stress or aversive stimuli. Scoring high in neuroticism scales means that the individual is emotionally reactive and susceptible to stress. They tend towards being loose and disrespectful in the way they express their emotions. They make a mountain out of small issues. More likely, they may misinterpret an ordinary situation and see it as a threat. It becomes hopelessly tricky for them when they encounter minor frustrations.

Neuroticism is interlinked with a defeatist attitude and being pessimistic towards work, apparent anxiety towards work, and the confidence that work hinders personal relationships. Scoring high in neuroticism is connected with a high possibility to show skin-conductance reactivity, with diminished ability to regulate emotions which affects one's capability to think with clarity, make sound choices and deal with stress effectively. People who score high in neuroticism lack contentment with their achievements in life and have a high chance of falling into clinical depression. They tent to go through more negative life events; their psychological wellbeing is worse off.

On the other hand, those scoring less on neuroticism are hardly annoyed and have less emotional reactivity. They are usually calm and have emotional stability. They do not experience persistent negative feelings.

Conscientiousness

This personality type is marked with the ability to show self-discipline. Individuals in this category have a strong sense of duty and strive to achieve without paying much attention to external expectations or measures. They are excellent planners, focused on achievement, dependable, and disciplined. They understand how to regulate, control, and give direction to their impulses. Stubbornness and focus are associated with high conscientiousness.

Low conscientiousness is perceived as being flexible, freewheeling, and spontaneous, but sometimes it can appear as a lack of reliability and sloppiness and may tend to be careless. It is a helpful personality trait and has been connected to better achievement in school and the workplace.

With such knowledge, you can interact with a person for a while, interpret, and tell the type of personality they have.

Chapter 3 Feet and Legs

When engaging in a conversation, we typically don't pay attention to the movements of the lower body. Since our direct line of sight is from the chest up, we often miss the obvious signs of the legs and feet. Certain stances that occur within the legs can signify dominance, sexual attraction, and even anxiety. Let's consider a few common patterns to look for when attempting to analyze someone else.

Crossed Legs

Crossed legs could indicate defensiveness. Perhaps you are sitting in a meeting at work, and your colleague says something totally off-putting. You may find yourself slowly crossing your legs as a subliminal way of showing your disapproval. Defensiveness could be heightened when one hand is positioned on top of the crossed leg. This is almost like a taunting move, signaling combat.

Crossing the ankles or knees are signs of nervousness, anxiety, and fear. This stance is protective in nature, which indicates that someone is attempting to protect themselves from whatever source of fear they are encountering. It could also be a means to control actions during high adrenaline situations.

Pointing and Active Legs

If you are miserable at a party, likely your legs are pointed towards the door as you are ready to leave. Our legs inadvertently point to where our heart wants to go. This can be used to determine interest and attraction. The legs, even when covered, will almost always point in the direction they are interested in.

Legs that bounce continuously could mean two things: boredom and nervousness. When you witness a person continuously bouncing their legs up and down, they may be nervous about something. This bounce is like a protective blanket that distracts their mind from their jitters. In addition, when someone is growing restless and ready to go, they may move their legs rapidly. The bouncing or tapping of the legs can be likened to a compulsion carried out to make the irritation subside.

When both legs point in one direction, it could be a clear indicator of interest for the person. However, when one leg steps back, it could indicate that the person wants distance. They may be uncomfortable with the person, conversation, or situation at hand. This subtle movement could be their way of escaping something distressful.

Messages from the Thighs

The upper portions of the legs usually indicate sexual or suggestive invitations between men and women. In daily activities, men may sit with their thighs opened as a sign of dominance. This outward display of masculinity represents an "alpha male" mentality. With women, closed thighs are a polite sign of femininity. Many young girls are instructed to sit with their legs closed so as not to expose their private areas. This closed manner of sitting is graceful and emanates class. When opened, they express dominance and even a form of female rebellion. Since it is so common for girls to be taught to keep their legs closed, doing the opposite could indicate opposition to societal norms. In addition, it is also extremely flirtatious to sit with the thighs crossed and one sitting higher above the other. This could indicate interest.

The Feet

The feet work very closely with the legs to determine areas of interest. When the toes are pointed at a specific object or direction, this indicates where we want to go. This could be a subtle signal your body sends to your mind about certain situations. The feet are used to make a statement and could also be used as an accent to verbal cues. Stomping, imaginative kicking, or tapping are all means of gaining attention.

When toddlers throw tantrums, it's not only their flailing arms, crying eyes, and yelling demands that occur. Toddlers utilize their legs and feet to create loud noises to further emphasize their anger.

Much like moving the legs, bouncing the feet or excessive pacing are signs of anxiety. During moments of high adrenaline, the feet can be seen moving uncontrollably, almost like rabbit's feet. Signs of nervousness are also present when the feet are curled behind an object, perhaps the legs of a chair or a table. Since curving the body inward is a subtle sign of inner protection, the feet follow suit with this protective stance.

Professor Geoffrey Beattie of the University of Manchester reveals that subtle foot movements and positioning could reveal signs of personality traits. He explains, "The weird thing about feet is that most people know what they are doing with their facial expressions; they may or may not know what they are doing with their hands, but unless we specifically think about it, we know nothing about what we are doing with our feet." Through his studies, he found that individuals with rather arrogant or haughty personalities typically kept their feet still as they were always aware of the self; whereas, shy individuals frequently shuffled their feet when sitting. This gives us insight into the characteristics of a person. Typically, shy people indicate high levels of nervousness or anxiety during social occasions. This directly proves the notion that foot movement equals anxiety. The beauty behind interpreting subtle body movements is that you can always find a glimmer of proof to solidify the theory.

Feet are also directly related to laughter. When we are extremely tickled by something, our feet come slightly off the ground. We may even partner that laughter with a slap of the knee. Dr. Beattie mentioned that men and women subconsciously show their attraction by combining feet movement during laughter. This indicates that the woman is comfortable enough with you to make obvious movements. As far as men, he says, "With men, feet aren't so important.

When it comes to interpreting the signs of the legs and feet, direction and movement are the two primary components needed for translation. Although we typically fret from glancing at the bottom half of a person, simple movements could be a key indicator as to how a person is feeling. It's imperative to understand the beauty of intricate movements in order to fully understand the inner workings of another person.

Chapter 4 Torso

Body Posture

Expectedly, posture, and body orientation should be interpreted in the context of the entire body language to develop the full meaning being communicated. Starting with an open posture, it is used to denote amicability and positiveness.

In this open position, the feet are placed openly, and the palms of the hands are facing outward. Individuals with open posture are deemed more persuasive compared to those with other stances.

To realize an open stance, one should stand upright or sit straight with the head upright and maintain the abdomen and chest bared. When the open posture is combined with an easy facial expression and good visual contact, it makes one look approachable and composed. Maintain the body facing forward toward the other person during a conversation.

There is also the closed posture where one crosses the arms across the chest or crosses the legs or sits in a facing a forward position as well as displaying the backs of the hands and closing the fists are indicative of a closed stance.

The closed posture gives the impression that one is bored, hostile, or detached. In this posture, one is acting cautious and appears ready to defend themselves against any accusation or threat.

For the confident posture, it helps communicate that one is not feeling anxious, nervous, or stressed. The confident posture is attained by pulling oneself to full height, holding the head high, and keeping the gaze at eye level. Then bring your shoulders backward and keep the arms as well as legs to relax by the sides. The posture is likely to be used by speakers in a formal context such as when making a presentation, during cross-examination and during project presentation.

Equally important, there is postural echoing and is used as a flirting technique by attracting someone in the Guardian. It is attained by observing and mimicking the style of the person and the pace of movement. When the individual leans against the wall, replicate the same.

By adjusting your postures against the others to attain a match, you are communicating that you are trying to flirt with the individual. The postural echoing can also be used as a prank game to someone you are familiar with and often engage in casual talk.

Maintaining a straight posture communicates confidence and formality. Part of the confidence of this posture is that it maximizes blood flow and exerts less pressure on the muscle and joints, which enhances the composure of an individual. The straight posture helps evoke desirable mood and emotion, which makes an individual feel energized and alert. A straight posture is highly preferred informal conversations such as during meetings, presentation, or when giving a speech.

Correspondingly being in a slumped position and hunched back is a poor posture and makes one be seen as lazy, sad, or poor. A slumped position implies a strain to the body, which makes the individual feel less alert and casual about the ongoing conversation.

On the other hand, leaning forward and maintaining eye contact suggests that one is listening keenly. During a speech, if the audience leans forward in an upright position, then it indicates that they are eager and receptive to the message.

Furthermore, if one slants one of the shoulders when participating in a conversation, then it suggests that the individual is tired or unwell. Leaning on one side acutely while standing or sitting indicates that you are feeling exhausted or fed up with the conversation and are eagerly waiting for the end or for a break.

Think of how you or others reacted when a class dragged on to almost break time. There is a high likelihood that the audience slanted one of their shoulders to left or right direction. In this state, the mind of the individual deviates to things that one will do next. In case of a tea break, the mind of the students will deviate to what one will do during or after the tea break.

By the same measure standing on one foot indicates that one is feeling unease or tired. When one stands on one foot, then it suggests that the person is trying to cope with uncomforting. The source of uneasiness could be emotional or physiological.

For instance, you probably juggled your body from one foot to help ease the need to go for a short call or pass wind. It is a way to disrupt the sustained concentration that may enhance the disturbing feeling.

If one cups their head or face with their hands and rests the head on the thighs, then the individual is feeling ashamed or exhausted.

When the speaker mentions something that makes you feel embarrassed, then one is likely to cup their face or head and rest the face on the thighs. It is a literal way of hiding from shame.

Children are likely to manifest this posture though while standing. When standing this posture may make one look like he or she is praying.

Additionally, if one holds their arms akimbo while standing, then the individual is showing a negative attitude or disapproval of the message. The posture is created by holding the waist with both hands while standing up straight and facing the target person. The hands should simultaneously grip on the flanks, the part near the kidneys. In most cases, the arms-akimbo posture is accompanied by disapproval or sarcastic face to denote attitude, disdain, or disapproval.

When one stretches both of their shoulders and arms and rests them on chairs on either side, then the individual is feeling tired and casual. The posture is akin to a static flap of wings where one stretches their shoulder and arms like wings and rests them on chairs on either side. It is one of the postures that loudly communicates that you are bored, feeling casual, and that you are not about the consequences of your action.

The posture is also invasive of the privacy and space of other individuals and may disrupt their concentration.

If one bends while touching both of their knees, then the individual is feeling exhausted and less formal with the audience. The posture may also indicate extreme exhaustion and need to rest.

For instance, most soccer players bend without kneeling while holding both of their knees, indicating exhaustion. Since in this posture, one is facing down, the posture may be highly inappropriate in formal contexts and may make one appear queer.

When one leans their head and supports it with an open palm on the cheeks, then it indicates that one is thinking deep and probably feeling sad, sorrowful or depressed.

The posture is also used when one is watching something with a high probability of negative outcomes such as a movie or a game. The posture helps one focus deep on the issue akin to meditating.

Through this posture, an individual try to avoid distractions and think deeper on what is being presented.

If you watch European soccer, you will realize that coaches use this posture when trying to study the match, especially where their team is down. However, this posture should not be used in formal contexts as it suggests rudeness. The posture should be used among peers only.

Then there is the crossing of the legs from the thigh through the knee while seated on a chair, especially on a reclining chair. In this posture, one is communicating that he or she is feeling relaxed and less formal.

In most cases, this posture is exhibited when one is at home watching a movie or in the office alone past working hours. If this posture is replicated in a formal context, then it suggests boredom or lack of concentration.

For the posture where one crosses the legs from the ankle to the soles of the feet while seated, it communicates that one is trying to focus in an informal context such as at home. For instance, if a wife or a child asks the father about something that he has to think through, then the individual is likely to exhibit this posture. If this posture is replicated in a formal context, then it suggests boredom or lack of concentration.

Torso

As the legs take up quite a portion of the body, they can also force the torso to lean certain ways. This is an added means of reading the nonverbal messages that the legs are giving out.

Our torso is a substantial body part that we communicate through. When you think of body language, you probably think of somebody's face, how they use their arms, or maybe the way that they use their legs.

The torso has specific signals that matter as well. Within your chest are the rest of the critical parts of your body. While your head is like the control center, it's pointless if everything else doesn't work. You could lose an arm or a leg and still be perfectly able to survive. You would not be able to drop your stomach or your heart, because you wouldn't be able to function, you could get a transplant, of course, but our bodies cannot live without these things. This means that this is a part of our body that we are going to protect the most.

Your brain is going to focus on making sure that if you feel uncomfortable. As mentioned before, you might cross your arms as a way to protect your torso.

We have to remember that this is going to show through our body language more than most subconscious movements. You're making certain moves to try and protect this part of your body. For example, somebody might curl up in the fetal position with their arms over their chests. This is because they're trying to comfort themselves and feel a little bit more protected.

Chapter 5 Arms

Arms, Hands and Fingers

Your hands are the gateway to communicating your feelings to the world. People tend to focus more on the slightest movement of the hands and fingers as compared to the rest of the body. Why? It boils down to evolution once again. As humans evolved and moved to an upright position, the hands have become more expressive, skilled, and also more dangerous.

Therefore, we tend to focus more on the hand movements to gauge what people are saying and to see if they have bad intentions. People find those with expressive use of hand movement as persuasive and of high credibility.

The Appearance of the Hand Speaks Volumes

It is relatively easy to assess a person's line of work by looking at their hands. The hands of an individual who spends all day typing on a system will often have a dainty and slender look. On the other hand, laborer's hand will have a certain rough and calloused appearance.

A pianist or guitarist is likely to have calluses on the fingers. Athletes are likely to have more scars than most people.

The way people take care of their hands is also an important factor to consider when dealing with people. An individual with perfectly manicured long nails is perceived as someone who values social conventions. Nail-biting is often seen as a sign of nervousness or insecurity.

Analyze People through Their Handshakes

Have you ever shaken hands with someone, and it felt as if your hand was being crushed? Perhaps you've been put off by a weak and "limpy" handshake before? Some people don't realize that the power to make a good impression resides in their hands since it's often the first point of physical contact with another person.

The handshake is a defining moment in your relationship with another. It will give you a first-hand feel of the person you are dealing with.

Certain people have decided to turn a simple handshake into an opportunity to assert dominance, which can be annoying since it is an intentional ploy to subdue the other party. Some go a little further by employing the "politician's handshake," which involves using the left hand to cover a handshake. These types of handshakes tend to alienate rather than make a good impression.

Take Note of Cultural Differences

In the Middle East, for instance, it is a sign of respect when two men hold hands together for long periods. You are likely to meet uncomfortable stares if you attempt this in Western cultures.

If you are planning to travel to new places, try to understand the culture and norms of your destination. If someone from the Middle East region and some parts of Asia wants to hold your hand, let them! Don't be surprised if your Russian male host kisses you on the cheek. Don't rebuff these gestures since it warms people up to you and makes them easier to analyze.

Analyzing Nonverbals of the Arms

Up to now, we have examined the importance of appearance and the way our hand movements dictate our credibility. Now let's examine nonverbals of the arms that will help us know what others are feeling and thinking.

Offensive Hand Displays

Finger Pointing

In many countries, finger pointing is seen as a very offensive and distasteful hand gesture. It is the cause of many fights in schools, prison yards, and on the streets. People focus more on the hostile message of the finger-pointing gesture than your verbal statement at that moment.

This is one of the reasons why parents are advised not to use these gestures when communicating with their kids. In addition to that finger-pointing, snapping your fingers in people's faces is regarded as disrespectful and rude.

High-Confidence Hand Display

These hand displays reflect the high degree of assurance and self-confidence an individual is feeling. Here are a few high-confidence hands displays to watch out for in people.

Insecure Hand Displays

Here's a counterpart to the high-confidence hand displays. The low-confidence or insecure hand displays are accurate reflections of the brain's insecurity, discomfort, and self-doubt. So let's examine some hand behaviors that reflect this state.

Frozen Hands

According to research, liars tend to show fewer nonverbal gestures than honest people. When we lie or feel cornered or insecure, we tend to move less or perhaps freeze in order not to draw attention.

It's very easy to detect frozen hands since the person's hand gestures become restrained while telling a lie. So, look out for these restrained hand gestures since they reveal a lot about what's going on in the person's brain.

Hand Wringing

It is usually a sign of stress or low confidence when people interlace their fingers or wring their hands. These are the common responses people use to calm themselves when they feel under stress, threatened, or have low confidence about a situation. The hand-wringing increases in intensity as issues get worse or difficult.

Hand Rubbing

We tend to rub the palms of our hands together when they feel cold; it is a way to warm them up. The lower the temperature, the faster the intensity of the hand rubbing.

This hand gesture is also used by those who are in doubt or under stress. Rubbing the hands together is a way of reassuring or pacifying the brain from doubts and negative emotions that you feel. As the situation escalates, an individual will progress from hand rubbing to interlocking of the fingers.

Emphatic Gestures

How often do we say, "If I were you," and I mean in reality, "If I, I were in one place like yours...?" It's not easy to feel what it's like in someone else's shoes. What do you think of the following rule?

Someone who cannot become aware of their own body language signals will never be able to register the signals of others very accurately. Body language analysis requires not only a "sharp" (read: trained) gaze and a "good" (i.e. trained) ear, but probably a much higher degree of good "sense."

This word describes a good empathy without which any method of self and human knowledge will fail. (You may also know someone who has attended 30 seminars and has read 500 books on the subject and yet does not get beyond a certain limit?) Registering one's own feelings and non-verbal signals means going through two essential processes:

First, one perceives a signal, e.g. For example, one tugs nervously on the lip. Second, you register how you feel right now. This combination helps one later tote others guess what feeling may have triggered a certain signal with them. Of course, this guessing is commonly called 'interpret' because it sounds 'scientific'. However, the fact remains that scientists must also "guess" as long as they work on a theory of knowledge, that is, create. Empathy for others can, therefore, be practiced by registering one's own processes. We can express this again as a rule:

The more empathy a person has with their own emotional world, the more they will be able to develop for others.

And vice versa. This rule also explains why especially sensitive people not only much understanding for others but are also overly sensitive (sometimes mimosa-like) to others. Suggestive Gestures

Suggestive Gestures

Studies show that the way you hold your palms will say a lot about you.

When you have your palms facing upwards, you will show a positive behavior while palms facing downwards will show negative behavior.

Palms facing up tell the person that you are welcoming and honest.

For example, if you are negotiating with a salesperson when buying something and he is putting his palms facing upwards while saying he cannot go any lower than he is honest, and you need to believe him.

If the palms are facing downwards, then he is more emphatic.

It has also been known that those who talk without gesticulating are prone to talking lies than those that talk with a lot of gestures.

If you have watched a politician talk, then you must have realized that they usually use a lot of gestures than many people.

They also like to use open arm gestures to show some honesty.

Pointing is rare in most cases with politicians because they know that it is seen to be rude.

Prompting Gestures

Verbal and nonverbal cues determine how well you can communicate with people. It is about understanding the content and the context at the same time and communicating back in kind. Verbal cues are simple prompts in conversation that ask for your attention or need your response to something. They are very clear.

"Does anyone have the answer?"

This is a direct verbal cue prompting anyone who might have the correct answer to speak up. Everyone understands this. If you don't have the answer, you might probably look around the room to see who has so that you can be attentive and listen to their explanation. Verbal cues are straightforward and explicit. You cannot mistake them.

Direct verbal cues are clear, whether you are asking a question or giving instructions. The message is clear between the decoder and the sender of the message. There is a chronological order in which ideas are conveyed.

The difference with nonverbal cues? These are indirect. They are often implied but not explicit. Indirect verbal cues can be subtle. You have to be very keen to identify them. Given their complicated nature, they are often easy to misunderstand.

Indirect verbal cues are often affected by context. Instead of saying what they want, someone acts it out, hoping you can understand them without them having to say it out loud. Affiliation to different cultural groups, societies, and other interactions often affect the understanding of indirect verbal cues. It might not be easy to read verbal cues, but with some insight, you can hack it. Here are some useful tips:

Recognize Differences. You must first understand that people are different, and for this reason, their communication styles might not be similar to yours. Everyone responds to verbal cues differently. When you respect this, it is easier to create an environment where you can understand one another.

Overcoming Bias. The next thing you have to overcome is your personal bias. Everyone is biased over something in one way or the other. Most of the time, you are biased without even realizing it. This is because of inherent traits, beliefs, and core values that you live by. These affect the way you comprehend things or how you recognize challenges.

Some people who are used to direct verbal cues might find it difficult to interact with people who are used to indirect verbal cues. You might even assume them dishonest because they are not communicating in a manner you are used to. On their part, they might find you unassuming, difficult to deal with, and insensitive. Some might even feel offended, yet you both mean well.

Embrace Diversity. Effective communication is about embracing diversity. People show different emotions in different ways in different parts of the world. This might not be the same as what you are used to, but it is how they do things. It is wise to learn about cultural relations, especially if you might have a very diverse audience.

Practice. You can learn everything you don't know. Learning means setting aside time to practice and get used to people, styles, and so forth. Learning will help you to become flexible and understand the differences between your preferred style of communication and another person's.

Chapter 6 Face

Facial Expressions

Your face is only one small part of your body, but it has a massive impact on what people will be able to pick up from you. While your face might be smaller than something like your stomach or the rest of your body as a whole, it's still an important part that can express a lot of very crucial signals to the person that you're communicating with. People will often look at your face more than anything. They want to look in your eyes, at your mouth and get a better understanding of what you're trying to share. Let's take a look at all the ways that your facial expressions can share greater truth about you in yourself.

Importance of Eyes

We say that the eyes are a window into the soul. That's pretty true; our eyes give a ton of information away about us. Most animals will communicate through eye contact. Our eyes are the one thing that we use to see what's around us and how we pick up on different situations. Let's first discuss what looking up might mean.

How many times have you simply looked up, but somebody else accused you of rolling your eyes? This can be a sign of discomfort. Our eyes will look for the things that are the most interesting around us. If you're having a more challenging conversation and you start to shift your eyes back and forth. When a person looks up, it can often be because they're only looking for more information. They're looking around themselves, trying to either escape the situation by picking up on something to change the subject, or they're searching their brain for more knowledge to include in this interaction.

Looking up can also indicate that we might be trying to recall different types of information. Looking to the left or right could give a signal to the other person that we are lying.

The squinting of the eyes means that we might be trying to focus on something a little more precisely. You'll have to look at the gaze and how long it might be so that people can better understand what the intention of that glare might be. Frequently, we are just like kids are like animals where if we see something shiny or pretty out of the corner of our eyes, we're going to look. It's just a natural human instinct to want to see things that are around us. To use positive eye movements on other people, you can try to notice glances. You might glance at something across the room that you want them to look at as well. Our eyes do a lot of talking to the other person without us even realizing it. If you look at something across the room, then they might be more likely to look at it as well. Alternatively, think about how somebody else might look across the room, and then you also look in that same direction. It's merely a way of our minds thinking that there's something more attractive now than when you got in the room.

Even subtle glances that are less than a second can be an indication that somebody is thinking about something else. For example, if you're having a conversation with somebody and they glance rather quickly right at the front door, then it could be a sign that they're getting bored and that they want to leave. They might look at a clock because they're feeling as though time is passing too slowly. They might glance down with their hands because they're not interested in what you're talking about and are trying to distract themselves.

Pay attention to how people use their eyes, but also consider where they're looking in the context of the location so you can better understand the intention of their eyes.

Micro expressions

Micro expressions are tiny little features within our face that give us a better indication of what somebody else might be thinking or wanting to do. Whether it's a small wrinkle in their forehead or the way that they move their mouth, we can start to pick up on these tiny micro expressions to better understand what somebody is really thinking inside their head.

There are seven different emotions that we can pick up through micro expressions. These include anger, fear, disgust, sadness, content, happiness, and surprise.

These micro expressions will show people in different ways. However, there are specific indications that we can use, which will help us better understand what somebody might be feeling.

Let's first discuss anger. Anger is something that we can pick up on by the way that a person uses their eyebrows and their mouth.

If eyebrows are pointed down and inwards towards the nose, then this is a sign of anger. The lower lid might also become raised up and closing over their eyes, in a way that makes their lives look a little bit more squinted. They'll often keep their lips sucked in and tight around their mouths.

They might have a frown in the way that their cheeks are tense, and their mouths are pointing downwards. Let's move on then to discuss something that we do when something might smell bad, or if we simply don't like the information that somebody is telling us.

We can show disgust in the same kind of way that we do anger in terms of eyebrow usage. Disgust will often leave the person with their mouth hanging open a little bit more. They'll have tense cheeks and a wrinkled nose. Their face is basically recoiling away from the disgusting thing that they're hearing.

Fear is going to have similar eyebrow movements as well. However, they'll be raised extremely high and flat.

If somebody's forehead is wrinkled, and their mouth is slightly open, then this can also tell us that they are feeling fear. Look at the rest of their body to indicate if it's fear, or if it's just surprise. Surprise looks a lot like fear but a little bit more positively. When somebody is surprised, they'll have curved eyebrows versus flat eyebrows as when they're fearful. They'll have their mouth open, but they might have the corners of their mouth turned up a little bit as well.

Even when we receive bad news, we can still sometimes have a smile. The smile might manifest simply because we're trying to work through that emotion in our brain. Sadness is like anger turned downwards. You'll have those arched eyebrows; except they'll be hanging a little bit looser and closer to your eyes.

A more relaxed cheek is seen in sadness, but the corners of their mouth will also be turned down. Content is sort of like complacency. You're satisfied with the moment, but you're not necessarily happy. You feel comfortable, and you're not really angry or anything like that. Content is when we keep our mouths flat. You might have one side or the other raised. Not in a smile just sort of half expression.

This is because we don't have that much emotion at the moment, but we're trying to show the other person what that emotion might be in our face.

The Influence of Smiles

Fake smiling is frequent because it's a way to make the other person know that we're okay with what's going on, but we might not necessarily fully be feeling that emotion.

You can tell somebody is fake smiling by what their eyes look like. Somebody who is fake smiling is not going to have any wrinkles in their eyes, and their eyebrows are going to be completely normal. Somebody who is genuinely smiling will have slightly raised eyebrows and lines in the corners of their eyes.

While their mouth might look the exact same, it's the top of their face that you can use to determine whether somebody's smile is genuine or not.

There are some studies that show that smiling can make you look younger, thinner, and generally like a more exciting person. Those who smile more might actually live longer. We need to conduct more research to really determine if this is the truth or if it's just coincidence. However, some research has helped us realize that people do tend to have longer lifespans based on how much more they might be smiling.

When somebody is smiling, and their mouth is slightly open, then you know that they're thrilled. However, if they're smiling and their mouth is free, and they are genuinely using their eyes, it could be a sign of fear or anxiety. They might be feeling comfortable, but they're using a smile to try to suit the situation. What we have to understand about smiles more than anything else, is that the other person might not be actually that happy but they're at least letting us know that they're feeling generally good. A smile can be a potent tool so you should learn all the ways you can show one. Practice smiling in the mirror to make it look more genuine. Fake smiling isn't always the greatest if you're in a personal relationship. However, a smile can really help in a business and professional setting, it makes everybody feel better, more relaxed, calmer, and more collected (Selig, 2016).

Head Movements

Your head is one of the most critical parts of your body. It has your brain inside of it after all. At the same time, our head can tell us a ton about how we might be feeling. Notice the way that somebody uses their head when they're talking to you.

A head turned downwards can be a way of actually protecting your neck and your chin from getting hurt. It can be a subconscious way of protecting the jugular to make sure that no outside threat could kill you. This is done sometimes when we might be angry, sad, or fearful in general as a way of trying to protect ourselves. Notice the idea that someone is using their eyes when they might be turning their head down as well. If their head is down and they're looking up at you, then they might simply just be tired and want to rest. If their head is down and they're looking from left to right, it can be a sign of fear. If their head is down and they're looking down, it might be a sign that they're sad or depressed.

Notice the way that they turn their heads too. Our leaders can tell us a lot about what is most interesting to us, though we might often turn our entire bodies towards the thing that is causing intrigue.

Somebody who's tilting their head from side to side might also be showing you that they're interested in what you're talking about. They can also be trying to make you feel more comfortable and using it as a way to be a little bit more flirtatious. Nodding or shaking is another powerful way that we use our heads. Those who bow in approval will frequently be in agreement with what you're saying.

Disapproval is going to be from left to right. Even if somebody is actively saying, "Yes," they agree out loud, they might still be nodding their head up and down. It could be a sign of encouragement and that we are still in approval.

But if it's left to right, then it might be a sign of their true feelings that they're trying to hide from you again. Consider cluster movements and notice the head in conjunction with micro expressions. This will give you the most authentic insight into how somebody might be trying to use their body.

Chapter 7 Voice

Tone

The tone, volume, pitch, and emphasis of a person's voice can help you decode the hints that can help you tell what they are feeling. For example, if you notice plenty of inconsistencies in the tone of their voice as they speak, they are probably very angry, hurt, excited, or nervous. Ever notice how your voice shakes when you speak in a rage or are nervous about something? It can also be a sign the person is lying.

Similarly, if a person is speaking louder or softer than their regular volume, something may be amiss. Again, a person's tone is a dead giveaway. Sometimes people say something that sounds like a compliment. However, upon examining their tone closely, you realize the sarcasm and the condescension with which it was uttered.

The tone in which an individual ends their sentence says a lot about what they are trying to convey even with similar verbal clues. For example, if a person completes their sentence on a raised note, they are doubtful of something or are asking a question. Similarly, if they finish the sentence with a flat tone, they are pronouncing a statement or judgment. Watch out for how people end their sentences to get a clue about their inner feelings.

Again, the words people emphasize can help you uncover their true feelings. For example, if a person says, "Have you borrowed the blazer?" while emphasizing 'borrowed,' it indicates their doubt over whether you have borrowed, stolen, or done something else to the blazer. However, if the emphasis is on 'you,' they aren't sure if it is you or someone else who has borrowed the blazer.

I also like to look at pauses between phrases to know about the person's attitude, emotions, and intentions. For example, if a person pauses after saying something, it could be because what they just said is extremely important to them, or they truly believe in it. Sometimes, a person pauses to seek validation or feedback from others. The speaker wants to gauge your reaction to what they said since it is important for them.

When people are in a more emotionally unstable or negative frame of mind (angry, hurt, or upset), their voice tends to be higher pitched or squeaky. They are most likely losing a grip on their emotions or aren't able to regulate their emotions effectively, notice how, when people are very angry, their voice becomes more screechy and squeakier, as if they are about to cry.

The speed of a speech

A person's emotions clearly impact the speed of their speech. Notice how you start talking much faster than your normal rate of speech, or words per minute, when you are angry or upset. A rapid speech can convey lack of organization, uncertainty, or lack of clarity. The person is not very comfortable with speaking and is just trying to finish throwing his or her words. Again, a slower than usual pace translates into low self-confidence, inability to express emotions, inability to come to terms with one's emotions, lack of emotional reassurance, and other similar feelings.

Chapter 8 Universal Non-verbal Signs

Non-verbal communication will be different for everyone, and it is in different cultures. A person's cultural background will define their non-verbal communication because some types of communication, such as signals and signs, have to be learned.

Because there are various meanings in non-verbal communication, there can be miscommunication could happen when people of different cultures communicate. People might offend another person without actually meaning to because of the cultural differences. Facial expressions are very similar around the world.

There are seven micro-expressions that are universal, and they are content/hate, surprise, anger, fear, disgust, sadness, and happiness. It could also be different to the extent of how people show these feelings because, in certain cultures, people might openly show them where others don't.

You are an American, and you take a trip to Italy. You don't speak Italian. You don't take a translator with you, and you forgot your translation dictionary. You have to rely on non-verbal communication in order to communicate with others.

You found a nice quiet restaurant you want to try so you point at your selection on the menu. You pay your bill and leave. The workers nod at you as you leave being a satisfied customer.

There could be other times when things won't go as well due to non-verbal communication such as people not making eye contact, or they get offended when you do make eye contact.

Nods could also have various meanings, and this causes problems. Some cultures their people might not say "yes," but people from a different culture will interpret as "no."

If you nod in Japan, they will interpret it as you are listening to them.

Here are different non-verbal communications and how they differ in various cultures:

- Physical Space

People in various cultures will have different tolerances for the space between people. People from the Middle East like to be close together when they talk to others. Other people could be afraid to be close to others while talking.

Americans and Europeans don't have as much acceptance about people entering what they consider their physical space. This is even less when talking about Asians. Everyone will have their own personal space that they don't want others to enter. There are many cultures where close contact between strangers is very acceptable.

- Paralanguage

The way we speak constitutes what we talk about. Pitch, rhythm, volume, vocal tones, can speak more than what the words are actually expressing. Asian people can keep themselves from shouting because they have been taught from childhood that this isn't acceptable.

This is what is known as vocal qualifiers. Yelling, whining, and crying are vocal characterizations that can change the message's meaning. In certain cultures, giggling is a very bad gesture. There are several emotions that can be expressed through vocal differences but are all a part of a person's paralanguage.

- Facial Expressions

Our faces can show emotions, attitudes, and feelings. Cultures can determine the degree of these expressions. Americans will show emotions more than people from Asia.

Most facial expressions are the same throughout the world, but certain cultures won't show them in public. These meanings are acknowledged everywhere. Showing too much expression can be taken as being shallow in certain places where others take it as being weak.

- Posture and Body Movement

People can get a message or information from the way your body moves. It can show how a person feels or thinks about you. If they don't face you when you are talking, it might mean that they are shy or nervous. It could also show that they really don't want to be talking with you. Other movements such as sitting far away or near someone could show that they are trying to control the environment. They might be trying to show power or confidence.

A person's posture such as sitting slouched or straight can show their mental condition. Having their hands in their pockets could show disrespect in various cultures. If you are in Turkey or Ghana, don't sit with your legs crossed as this is considered offensive.

- Appearance

This is another good form of non-verbal communication. People have always been judged for their appearance. Differences in clothing and racial differences can tell a lot about anyone.

Making you look good is an important personality trait in many cultures. What is thought to be good appearance will vary from culture to culture. How modest you get measured by your appearance.

- Touch

Touch can be considered rude in many cultures. Most cultures view shaking hands as acceptable. Hugs and kissing, along with other touches, are viewed differently in various cultures. Asians are very conservative with these types of communications.

Patting a person's shoulder or head has various meaning in different cultures, too. Patting a child's head in Asia is very bad because their head is a sacred piece of their body. Middle Eastern countries consider people of opposite genders touching as being very bad character traits.

How and where a person is touched can change the meaning of the touch. You have to be careful if you travel to different places.

- Gestures

You have to be careful with thumbs up because different cultures view it differently. Some could see it as meaning "okay" in some cultures but being vulgar in Latin America. Japan looks at is as money.

Snapping your fingers might be fine in some cultures but taken as offensive and disrespectful in others. In certain Middle Eastern countries, showing your feet is offensive. Pointing your finger is an insult in some cultures. People in Polynesia will stick out their tongue when they greet someone, but in most cultures, this is a sign of mockery.

- Eye Contact

Most Western cultures consider eye contact a good gesture. This shows honesty, confidence, and attentiveness. Cultures like Native American, Hispanic, Middle Eastern and Asian don't make eye contact as a good gesture. It is thought to be offensive and rude.

Unlike Western cultures that think it is respectful, others don't think this way. In Eastern countries, women absolutely can't make eye contact with men because it shows sexual interest or power. Most cultures accept gazes as just showing an expression but staring is thought to be rude in many.

Chapter 9 How to Spot Lie

Fact is that only 54% of the lies can be spotted in an accurate manner. Research has also proved that extroverts tell more lies when compared to the introverts and not less than 82% of the lies usually go without being detected.

However, the good news is that people can also improve their abilities for lie detection, maximizing to close to 90% accuracy. The big question here is how to detect that someone is lying. One of the initial steps in this whole process is getting with how someone typically acts, especially when they are speaking.

Basically, this is the process of coming up with known as a baseline. A baseline is essentially how a person acts when they are under non-threatening and just normal conditions. According to the Science of People website, it is basically how a person appears when they are saying the truth. To make it clearer, it might be a bit difficult to tell when a person is not speaking the fact if you are not sure of how they usually act when saying the truth, which, to a wider extent, makes a lot of sense.

However, the techniques that are used to determine if someone is lying can be very confusing. As a matter of fact, these strategies can even be very conflicting. Due to that, it is important to think twice before making an accusation, ensure that you feel more than once about doing it unless it is important to go ahead and find out what happened.

Here are some of the telltale signs that someone is not telling the truth.

The Behavioral Delay or Pause

It begins when you ask someone a question, and you get no reply initially. The person then begins to respond after some delay. There is one big question that should be asked here; how long should the delay extend before it becomes meaningful before it can be regarded as a deceptive sign? It, however, depends on a few factors. You can try this particular exercise on a friend, and ask a question like this, "What were you doing on a day like this six years ago.

After asking that question, you will notice that the person will take an invariable pause before answering the question. This is because it is not a type of question that naturally evokes a fast and immediate answer. Even as the person takes time to think about the question, he might still not be able to give a meaningful response. The next question to ask would be this," Did you rob a cloth shop on this day six years ago?" if they make a pause before giving you the answer you need, then it would be very important to pick the kind of friends you have wisely.

In most cases, there will be no pause, and the person is likely to respond by just saying no and letting the story die.

This is a simple test that tends to drive home the point that the delays should usually be considered out of the church of God. in the context of whether, it is appropriate for the question at hand.

The Verbal or Non-verbal Disconnect

The human brains have been wired in a manner that causes both the nonverbal and the verbal behaviors to match up in a natural manner. So, each time, there is disconnect it is usually regarded as a very important deceptive indicator. A very common verbal or nonverbal disconnect that you should look out for will occur when someone nods affirmatively while giving a "No" answer. It might also occur when a person moves his head from one end to the other when giving a "Yes" answer.

If you were to carry out that mismatch, as an example, to offer a response to a question, then you will realize that you will have to force yourself through the motion that you have. But despite all that, someone who is deceptive will still do it without even giving it a second thought.

There are a number of caveats that have been connected to this type of indicator. First of all, this type of indicator is not applicable in a short phrase or one-word response. Instead, it is only suitable in a narrative response. For instance, consider that a human head might make a quick nodding motion when a person says "No." That is just a simple emphasis and not a disconnect. Second, it is also very important not to forget that a nodding motion does not necessarily mean "Yes' in certain cultures. In such cultures, a side-to-side head motion also does not imply that the person is saying "No."

Hiding the Eyes or the Mouth

Deceptive people will always hide their eyes or mouth when they are not saying the truth. There is a tendency to desire to cover over a given lie, so if the hand of a person moves in front of their mouth while they are making a response to a given question, which becomes significant.

In a similar instance, hiding the eyes can be an inclination to shield a person from the outlast of those they could be lying to. If an individual shield or covers their eyes when they are responding to a question, what they could also be showing, on the level of subconscious, is that they can't bear to see the reaction to the lie they are saying. In most cases, this kind of eye shielding could be done using the hand, or the person could as well decide to close the eyes. Blinking is not in the picture here, but when a person closes their eyes while making a response to a question that doesn't need reflection to answer, which can be considered as a way of hiding the eyes, hence becoming a possible deceptive indicator.

Swallowing or Throat Clearing

If a person loudly swallows saliva or clears the throat before answering a given question, then there is a problem somewhere. However, if any of these actions are performed after they have answered the question, then there is nothing to worry about. But when it happens before answering a question, then there are some things that should be analyzed.

The person could be doing the nonverbal equivalent of the following verbal statements," I swear to God…" This is one of the ways of dressing the lie in the best attires before presenting it. Looking at it from the physiological point of view, the question might have created a type of anxiety spike, which can as well as cause dryness and discomfort in the throat and mouth.

The Hand-to-Face Actions

The other way of determining if someone is saying a lie is to check what they do with their faces or in the head region each time they are asked a question. Usually, this would take the form of licking or biting the lips or even pulling the ears or lips together. The main reason behind this reflects one of the simple science questions that are usually discussed in high school. When you have someone a question, and you notice that it creates a kind of spike in anxiety, what you should remember is that the right response will be damaging. In return, that will activate the autonomic nervous system to get to business and try to dissipate the anxiety, which might appear to drain a lot of blood from the surface of the extremities, ears, and the face. The effects of this could be a sensation of itchiness or cold. Without the person even realizing it, his hands will be drawn to the mentioned areas, and there could be rubbing or wringing of the hands. And just like that, you might have spotted a deceptive indicator.

The Nose Touch

Women usually carry out this special gesture with smaller strokes compared to those of men, as a way of avoiding smudging of their make-ups. One of the most important things to recall is that this kind of action should be read in context and clusters, as the person could have any hay of cold or fever.

According to a group of scientists at the Smell & Taste Treatment and Research Foundation that is based in Chicago, when someone lies, chemicals that are called catecholamine are released and make the tissue that is inside the nose to swell. The scientists applied a special imaging camera that reveals the blood flow in the body and show that deliberate lying can also lead to an increase in the blood pressure. This technology proves that the human nose tends to expand with blood when someone lies, and that is what is referred to as the Pinocchio Effect.

Maximized blood pressure will also inflate the nose and make the nervous nose tingle, leading to a kind of brisk rubbing with the hand to suppress the itching effect.

The swelling cannot be seen with the naked eyes, but it is usually what causes the nose touch gesture. The same phenomenon will also take place when a person is angry, anxious, and upset. American psychiatrist Charles Wolf and neurologist Alan Hirsch carried out a detailed analysis of the testimony of Bill Clinton to the Grand Jury on the affair he had with Monica Lewinsky. They realized that each time he was being honest, he rarely touched his nose. However, when he lied, he offered he appeared to be wearing a frown before he gave the answer and touched his nose once each 4 minutes for a mega total of 26 nose touches. The scientists also said the former US president didn't touch his nose at all when he offered the answers to the questions in a truthful manner.

A deliberate scratching or rubbing action, as opposed to a nose that could just be itching lightly, usually satisfies the itch of someone's nose. Usually, an itch is a repetitive and isolated signal and is out of context or incongruent with the general conversation of the person.

Eye Rub

When a child does not want to see something, the only thing they will do is to cover their eyes. They usually do this with both of their hands. On the other hand, when an adult does not want to see something distasteful to them, they are likely to rub their eyes. The eye is one of the attempts by the brain to block out a doubt, deceit, or any distasteful thing that it sees. It is also done to avoid looking at the face of the person who the lie is being said to. Usually, men would firmly rub their eyes, and they may look away if the myth is a real whopper.

Women are not so likely to use the eye rub gesture. Instead, they will use gentle and small touching emotions just beneath the eyes since they either want to avoid interfering with the makeups they are wearing, or they have been redesigned as girls to stay away from making several gestures. At times, they might also want to avoid the listener's gaze by trying to look away.

One of the commonly used phrases out there is lying through the teeth. It is used to refer to a cluster of gestures portraying fake smile and clenched teeth, accompanied by the famous eye rub.

Chapter 10 Spotting Romantic Interest

S potting romantic interest is one of the most popular topics of all time. Consistently, both men and women are interested in learning more about how they can determine if a person is genuinely attracted to them.

This topic is part science and part art. There is plenty of scientific evidence that backs up the reasoning behind attraction while there is an instinctive component, which cannot be adequately measured or quantified through scientific methods. What this implies is that if you are looking to gauge someone's level of attraction, then you need to have both a scientific approach and reliance on gut feelings.

To start things off, it should be noted that attraction works differently in men than it does in women. While the underlying biochemistry is essentially the same, the physical manifestations are different. In addition, cultural norms may govern romantic interactions to a varying degree.

In that regard, it is worth mentioning that while many of the non-verbal clues are the same, women tend to be a lot more subtle than men are. In contrast, most men tend to be very open about their feelings toward the object of their attraction. While this shouldn't be taken as a blanket statement, it is a general rule of thumb. After all, there are plenty of shy men out there who have trouble making their interest known while there are plenty of women who are quite overt about their feelings for the object of their interest.

One other note with regard to attraction is that romantic interactions are generally perceived to be between men and women.

That being said, I intend to have this discussion cover the entire spectrum of male and female interaction within a romantic context. That way, the information presented herein will provide you with the insights you need in order to improve your ability to pick up on the non-verbal clues indicating potential romantic interest and attraction.

Now, the first to keep in mind is that attraction is somewhat hard to define. The reason for this is that men and women seek different things in a potential mate. We are operating under the assumption that there is genuine attraction among those involved and not some hidden agenda spurring interest.

In that regard, the attraction is based on the qualities of an individual that meet or exceed the needs of the other. Hence, women tend to focus on different qualities in their potential romantic partner, whereas men tend to focus on a different set of qualities.

For instance, women tend to seek security and stability in a romantic partner. This is due to an instinctive need for survival and preservation of the species. In order to fully comprehend this, we would need to go all the way back to the day of primitive humans in which there was no guarantee that offspring would make it past their first year of life. As such, women, designated as a caregiver from the start, needed to secure the means and resources needed to ensure the survival of their offspring. On the other hand, the males were in charge of playing the role of provider.

In the early days of humankind, males were mainly hunter-gatherers. This means that they needed to go into the fray to find food. Whether food came from hunting or foraging, males were expected to provide the sustenance needed to ensure the survival of their offspring.

In contrast, males needed to find healthy females who had the physical qualities that would ensure their fertility and ability to bear children. I know that this sounds very primitive, but it is important to underscore this point as humans we are hardwired under this context. Consequently, thousands of years of evolution and biology are just now being challenged by the new social paradigm in which we find ourselves.

Over the last two hundred years or so, the dating paradigm has shifted dramatically.

Traditionally, most marriages were arranged. As such, it was not so much about love and romance, but about the position and financial stability. This paradigm lasted for a few centuries. Since the outset of the Industrial Revolution, the attitudes of society changed in such a way that men and women were free to choose who they wanted to marry. This opened the door for a number of circumstances.

So, men went from courting women to dating them. This meant that men needed to ensure that a woman would be willing to reciprocate his intentions and feelings. In contrast, women played a more passive role, and they were conditioned to wait for men to make the first move. However, they could drop subtle hints regarding their interest. That way, the man would be certain that he had a chance with a given woman.

In modern times, we are faced with a very liberal dating scene. While some countries have far more cultural and religious restrictions, most countries are fairly open about the manner in which they can pursue the object of their desire.

Consequently, it is imperative that both men and women gain deeper insight as to how attraction is expressed by either gender.

So, let us start off with men.

Men are a lot easier to read, as they tend to be far more overt about their interest in someone. They will generally seek the object of their interest and engage them in some manner. Typically, men will try to engage the other party by displays of strength, wealth, or status. These are signs that they are providers or protectors. In short, men try to position themselves as the best possible mate their object of interest can find.

Some general guidelines include direct eye contact, tilting their body toward the person they are attracted to and seeking constant physical contact. The latter generally tends to make most women uncomfortable, as unsolicited physical contact can get rather awkward quickly.

Other not so subtle hints that men drop are following the object of their affection around, placing their hands, or arms, as a sign of possession and frequent fidgeting. In fact, fidgeting is a dead giveaway as it is a sign that a man is nervous in the presence of whom they are attracted to.

In addition, some men might go silent (remember the freeze response?) and even fail to react in the presence of the object of the attraction. This reaction is partially due to the freeze response but it also due to the fact that some men freeze up when they don't know what to do or how to react.

This is why you see most dating advice that is oriented to men focus on what to do and what to say in various situations. What this does is that it eliminates a man's reliance on his wits by providing him with a set of tools. These tools are certainly useful though they may not be universally applicable.

One common method used by men is to approach and pull back. This method consists in approaching someone they are attracted to and then pulling away. Then, they will engage and withdraw until they are able to make progress, say, go on a first date. The logic beneath this approach is that men tend to come on very strong when they are attracted to someone. As such, this approach allows them to find a balance between displaying their intentions and giving the object of their attraction some space.

As you can see, men are far more open about their attraction toward someone based on the permissiveness that society has afforded men throughout history. However, women have been traditionally tagged with a more submissive role. Therefore, women are not always able to express their intentions overtly in the same way that men do.

Some not so subtle signs of attraction in women are eye contact, hair pulling, and trailing off in conversation.

When a woman is attracted to a person, she will seek eye contact. This eye contact tends to be rather brief as women are not interested in winning a staring contest. They just want to signal to the object of their interest that they are willing to be engaged.

Another telltale sign of attraction in a woman is related to her hair. If you see a woman playing or pulling on her hair when speaking to someone they like, you can be pretty sure that she is indicating a willingness to be engaged.

Also, women who are interested in a person will allow for closer physical contact. Any a time a woman keeps people at arms' length, it is a clear indication that they have no interest in them. By the same token, any time a woman avoids eye contact and tilts their body away from the person they is interacting with, it is safe to assume they are not interested in being engaged.

Women are generally focused on faces. What this means is that when a woman is attracted to someone, they will not only focus on their eyes but also their mouth. They generally tend to watch the other party's lips when they speak. This is an instinctive reaction based on their desire to find a strong and healthy mate. Consequently, healthy-looking eyes, teeth, lips, and skin are clear indicators that a person is in good physical condition.

Women also drop many hints with their arms and hands. A woman who is uninterested will almost always cross her arms and/or legs at some point. If you find that a woman is sitting in the manner on a date, then the other party has a tough time ahead for them.

Conversely, if a woman is actually interested in the other person, she will sit, or stand, in a very "open" position, that is, hands at her sides (or folded on a table) and legs uncrossed. Also, leaning forward while listening to the interlocutor is a good indication that they are interested in what the other person has to say. If they make direct eye contact on various occasions, then the combination of clues is virtually a declaration of intent.

Some women refrain from eye contact when they are genuinely attracted to someone. They may cross gazes but quickly look away or perhaps look down. In some cultures, this is the norm, as it is a sign of submission. Western cultures don't normally have such customs though women may still prefer to avoid eye contact in order to prevent themselves from being too obvious.

Finally, a woman's voice says a lot about the way she feels. Women tend to speak with a higher pitch when they are in the presence of someone they are attracted to. Also, they may raise the tone of their voice in order to be "noticed" by the person they are attracted to. In one on one interaction, don't be surprised if you see a woman speaking somewhat faster. However, if she begins to slow down, then that might very well be a signal that she has lost interest.

On the whole, men and women will exhibit very similar signs of attraction such as open lips, rounded eyes, eyebrows higher than usual and the classic pupil dilation (this is actually very hard to spot). However, hands, arms and body positioning are far more indicative of attraction than other signs commonly mentioned.

In addition, facial gestures such as smiling are good indicators though not foolproof. After all, you might be talking with someone who is upbeat and positive. However, that does not mean that they are attracted to you.

Chapter 11 Tips

Tips on How to Improve your Non-verbal Communication

Solid communication abilities can help you in both your own and expert life. While verbal and composed communication abilities are significant, investigate has shown that nonverbal practices make up an enormous level of our everyday relational communication.

How might you improve your nonverbal communication abilities? The accompanying tips can assist you with figuring out how to read the nonverbal signals of others and upgrade your own capacity to impart viably.

Focus on Nonverbal Signals

Individuals can convey data from numerous points of view, so focus on things like eye contact, gestures, posture, body developments, and manner of speaking. These signals can pass on significant data that isn't articulated.

By giving nearer consideration to others' implicit practices, you will improve your own capacity to convey nonverbally.

Search for Incongruent Behaviors

Research has indicated that when words neglect to coordinate with nonverbal signals, individuals will, in general, disregard what has been said and center rather around implicit expressions of states of mind, considerations, and feelings. So when somebody says a certain something, however, their body language appears to recommend something different, it tends to be valuable to give additional consideration to those unpretentious nonverbal signals.

Use Good Eye Contact

Great eye contact is another fundamental nonverbal communication ability. When people neglect to look at others without flinching, it can appear as though they are dodging or attempting to conceal something. Then again, an excessive amount of eye contact can appear to be fierce or threatening.

While eye contact is a significant piece of communication, recall that great eye contact doesn't always mean gazing steadily at someone. How you tell what amount of eye contact is right?

Some communication specialists suggest interims of eye contact enduring four to five seconds. Powerful eye contact should feel normal and agreeable for both you and the individual you are talking with.

Pose Inquiries About Nonverbal Signals

Occasionally, just posing such inquiries can loan a lot of clearness to a circumstance. For instance, an individual may be radiating sure nonverbal signals since he has something different on his mind. By inquisitive further into his message and plan, you may show signs of improvement thought of what he is truly attempting to state.

Use Signals to Make Communication More Meaningful

Recollect that verbal and nonverbal communication cooperate to pass on a message. You can improve your expressed communication by utilizing body language that strengthens and bolsters what you are stating. This can be particularly valuable when making introductions or when addressing an enormous gathering of individuals.

For instance, if you will probably seem sure and arranged during an introduction, you will need to concentrate on imparting nonverbal signs that guarantee that others consider you to be confident and competent. Standing solidly in one spot, shoulder back, and your weight-adjusted on the two feet is an extraordinary method to pause dramatically.

Take a gander at Signals as a Whole

Another significant piece of good nonverbal communication abilities includes having the option to adopt an increasingly all-encompassing strategy to what an individual is conveying. A solitary motion can mean any number of things, or possibly nothing by any means.

The way to precisely reading nonverbal conduct is to search for gatherings of signals that fortify a typical point. In the event that you place an excessive amount of accentuation on only one signal out of many, you may arrive at an off base decision about what an individual is attempting to state.

Think about the Context

At the point when you are speaking with others, generally consider the circumstance and the setting wherein the communication happens. A few circumstances require increasingly formal practices that may be deciphered contrastingly in some other setting.

Be Aware That Signals Can be Misread

As per somewhere in the range of, a confident handshake shows a solid character while a feeble handshake is taken as an absence of backbone. This model outlines a significant point about the plausibility of misreading nonverbal signals. A limp handshake may really show something different completely, for example, joint inflammation.

Continuously make sure to search for gatherings of conduct. An individual's general disposition is unmistakably more telling than a solitary signal saw in disengagement.

Practice, Practice, Practice

A few people simply appear to have a talent for utilizing nonverbal communication successfully and accurately deciphering signals from others. These individuals are regularly depicted as having the option to "read individuals."

As a general rule, you can fabricate this aptitude by giving careful consideration to nonverbal conduct and rehearsing various sorts of nonverbal communication with others. By seeing nonverbal conduct and rehearsing your own aptitudes, you can significantly improve your communication capacities.

Nonverbal communication abilities are fundamental and can make it simpler to pass on your point and to read what others are attempting to let you know. A few people appear to stop by these aptitudes normally, yet anybody can improve their nonverbal abilities with training.

Tips on How to protect yourself from Deception

It is relieving to know that there are defense mechanisms against deception and a person faced with a deceptive situation can always stand against and defend him/herself from it.

According to researchers, pride was one of the major factors that allow people to fall into deception. When a person feels he or she is too good and perfect, or feels he/she can be very careful, then it leaves room for the con agent to take advantage.

Enlightened skepticism is a technique used to defend yourself against deception, there is a saying: "truth fears no questions." This approach protects you from harmful forms of deception, as it is a way to assess the truth through a fact-finding and questioning method. When you do these things, you tend to gain from this effort in at least three ways, which are:

● You tend to hone your critical thinking skills.

● You learn to choose who to trust and to what extent to trust them.

● You get to find out who is after personal advantage at your expense.

In order to risk falling into someone's deceptive trap, researchers have come up with some enlightened skepticism questions that can help you to defend yourself against deception. Some of the questions to ask include:

1. What are the things I know about the person's truthfulness?

2. Is the person's statement consistent with the truth or reality?

3. Is there a way to verify or check the authenticity of the statement?

4. What do I stand to gain if I accept and act on the statement?

5. And if I don't gain, what would I lose if I accept and act on the statement?

6. What is the gain of the speaker if I buy into the statement?

7. Is there any part of the statement exaggerated or downplayed by the speaker?

8. Does the idea seem or sound too good to be true?

9. Would I advise my close relation to accept the statement without an iota of doubt?

10. What doesn't feel right?

These 10 questions make you more objective and allow you to think critically when receiving information. When you ask and answer these questions there is a lesser chance that you will be fooled since you will come across as sincere and sharp and this will ward off deceivers as they will move on in search of easier targets.

Just like simulations occur in deception, there is also simulation in defending or warding off the deception. These deception detection skills come with some fun simulations, some of which includes:

Talk shows on TV:

Listening to people argue about different topics. Pick out the truth, the exaggerations and half-truths told by a speaker in the process of making his/her point. Also, look out for outright lies, emotional reasoning, fallacies and all other deceptive behavior. Being able to identify these things allow you to get better at detecting deception.

Commercials: These also gives you opportunities to work more on your critical thinking skills. In advertisements there are a lot of mistakes in reasoning, arguments based on things without facts, a lot of lies and deception. Being able to detect this will improve your ability to detect a deceptive person from a distance.

If you can find the flaws in simulated information, hold on with judgment until you have enough information to render a reasonable accusation. It is only at this point that you can say that you have truly mastered the act of deceptive defense.

But again, a person who is good at defending him or herself from deception is only as good as the agent of deception he/she is faced with. Some people tend to be more skilled at lying and constant interaction and simulation are the only way to improve on one's deception detection.

Chapter 12 Deception

The method of mind control will have some parallels with manipulation in that manipulators will use a lot of deception to achieve their ultimate goal..

Deception is an act used by the agent to spread ideas in the object regarding facts that are falsehoods or that are just partial truths, along with subterfuge, mystification, hoax, provocation, and beguilement. Deception may include many different things like concealment, disguise, distraction, hand sleight, manipulation, and concealment. The agent will be able to control the subject's mind because the subject will trust them. The subject may believe what the agent says and may even base future plans and shape their life on the things the agent told them. Deception also happens in terms of relationships.

Types of Deception

Deception is a form of communication that relies on omissions and lies to persuade the subject to best fit the object of the environment. As contact is involved, several different types of deception may also occur. There are five different types of deception found, according to the Interpersonal Deception Theory. In the other forms of mind control, some of these have been seen, suggesting that there may be some overlap. The five main forms of deception are:

Lies: This is when the agent compiles data and provides information that is totally different from what the truth is. They can present that information as fact to the subject and the subject will see it as the truth. This can be risky, as the subject does not know that they are being fed false information; if the subject knew that the information is inaccurate, they would certainly not speak to the agent and there would be no deceit.

Equivocations: This is when the agent makes statements that are inconsistent, vague and indirect. This is intended to get the subject confused and not to understand what is happening. If the subject returns later and tries to blame them for the false information, it can also allow the agent to save face.

Concealments: This is one of the most commonly used forms of deception. Concealments are when the agent intentionally omits data relevant or important to the context and participates in any actions that would hide information relevant to the subject for that particular context. The agent is not likely to have lied explicitly to the subject, but they are going to make sure that the important information required never makes it to the subject.

Exaggeration: This is when the agent overestimates a fact or subtly twists the facts to turn the story the way they want. While the agent may not be lying explicitly to the subject, they are going to make the situation look like a bigger deal than it really is or they are going to change the reality a little so that the subject does what they want.

Understatements: An underestimate is the exact opposite of the method of exaggeration because the agent would downplay or diminish aspects of the reality. They are going to tell the subject that an event is not that big deal when it could actually be the thing that determines whether the subject gets to graduate or gets that big promotion.

These are just a few of the possible types of deception.

Motives for Deception

Researchers have shown that there are three main motives that are present in deceptions found in close relationships. These would include partner-focused motives, self-focused motives, and relationship focused motives.

Deception techniques

Camouflage

This is when the agent acts in a certain way to hide the truth so that the subject does not know that the information is missing. Often when the agent uses half-truths as they say information, it strategy will be used.

Disguise

The agent works to create the illusion of being something or someone else when this occurs. It is when the agent hides everything about themselves from the topic including their real name, what they are doing for a career, whom they have been with, and what they are up to when they go out. This goes beyond simply changing the outfit that someone wears in a play or film; when disguise is used in the process of deception, the agent attempts to change their entire persona to confuse and mislead the subject.

Simulation

It consists in displaying fake subject data. In simulation, there are three methods that can be used like deception, manufacturing, or mimicry. The agent may unintentionally represent something identical to itself in mimicry, and copying another template. They may have an idea similar to someone else's and they will assume it is all theirs instead of giving credit. By auditory, visual and other means, it type of simulation can often occur.

Fabrication is another method that can be used by the agent when using deception. What this means is that the agent is going to take something that is actually found and change it to be different. They can tell a story that has not happened or added to embellishments that make it sound better or worse than it was. While the core of the story may be true, yes, they got a bad grade on a test; some extra things are going to be put in as the teacher purposefully gave them a bad grade. The truth is that the agent has not been training, and that is why they first got the bad score.

Finally, in deception, distraction is another type of simulation. This is when the agent tries to get the target to focus their attention on something other than the facts; typically by baiting or providing something more enticing than the hidden truth.

Did I see ways in which I can improve in order to master or break free from one or more, if possible all 5 forms of dark psychology?

Have I outlined the necessary line of action to take?

Do I possess the discipline to stick to the line of action I have outlined?

If I should experience some shortcomings in following my outlined goals, how can I quickly get back on track?

Chapter 13 Body Language of Attraction

You may be insanely attracted to a person but may not have the courage to ask them out owing to the prospect of facing humiliation and rejection. Imagine how easier things would be if you knew if they are as much into you as you are into them. Think of a situation where you've been set up on a blind date by enthusiastic friends, or you find a date online, and really want to know if they are attracted to you. You may go out on a first date and come back not knowing whether the person really liked you or not!

Wouldn't it be nice if there could be a telepathic way to gauge if a person feels truly attracted to you? How can you figure out if a person is genuinely attracted to you or is being plain nice to you because they don't want to hurt you (yes, we've all been guilty of this.)

Can verbal and non-verbal clues help you establish a potential lover's true feelings, emotions, thoughts, and intentions? Can body language be used for unlocking a person's subconscious mind to tune in to their innermost feelings and thoughts about you? Use these secret attraction clues (that I rarely share with anyone) to help you gain and increase social proof and experience more gratifying and fulfilling relationships.

The Attraction Signals

When an individual is attracted to you, they will transmit plenty of feel-good or positive non-verbal clues for you to tune in to at a subconscious level.

To begin with, when a person is deeply attracted to you, their bodies will almost always face you.

Everything from their face, the chest to shoulders and feet will most likely be pointed in your direction. The person will lean closer while speaking or interacting with you in a bid to get closer on a subconscious and emotional level. When they stand at a distance of under four feet away from you, they are keen on entering or personal space or inner circle of friends. They are trying to physically enter your inner zone or personal space to make a place for themselves in it.

If you want to know if a person is keenly into you or interested in you, don't give in to their interest straight away. Rather than facing them, maintain a shoulder to shoulder position. If the person is truly interested in you, he or she will make an effort to win your attraction. Let them know that they have to win your attraction for you to stand facing them or mirror their attraction signals.

Leaning in the direction of a person is almost always a sign of attraction. We subconsciously lean towards people we are attracted to. When a person leans towards you in a group, it is clear that they are interested in you (or what you are speaking). Of course, sometimes a person may be simply keen on listening to what you are saying, in which case, you will have to look at other clues. However, leaning towards a person within a group setting is a subconscious indication that they are drawn towards you.

Another sign of attraction includes seizing a person from up to down, and then down to up. This is a primitive way, yet still practiced, for checking out the sexual potential of a prospective mate.

Together with other clues, uncrossed arms and legs can be a sign of attraction. Similarly, a broad smile, dilated pupils, and open palms can also reveal attraction. Head tilting is another sign of interest and engagement. It signals a person's desire to communicate to you that they are always around for you. Looking at a person in the eye for long while speaking can also be a huge sign of attraction. If you are attracted to a person or want to win their affection, avoid looking over their heads or even all over the place. It reveals a lack of interest and sensitivity, which will not give them the right signal.

Touch

Touch is a clue that an individual is completely comfortable in your presence. They may also be keen or getting to know more about you. They may get flirtatious or hit on you by playfully touching you. Some of the most common initial attractions signals are placing their hand over your hand, brushing their shoulder or leg against your shoulder or leg while talking to you and pretending to touch you accidentally.

If you are confused about how to read a person's touches, observe how they touch another person versus how they touch you. If they are generally touchy-feely with everyone around, it is their baseline personality.

However, if they make special exceptions in the manner in which they touch you, it is more often than not, a sign of attraction. If the individual touches more than normal or in a different way, he or she may be attracted to you.

If you are attracted to a person, use body language to your advantage by conveying your feelings through non-verbal signals. Don't distance yourself from the person even if you don't want to send out very obvious signs of attraction.

On a subconscious level, they may not realize they are attracted to you. Similarly, don't go all out and make the person step back in discomfort. Maintain a balance. Start with a light or playful tap on the shoulder or elbows. It is harmless yet reveals that a person likes you. Then gradually, move to touch their arm, wrist or back while talking. Make the touch more gradual and subtle so they don't wince or retreat with discomfort.

Mirroring

Mirroring happens at a deeply subconscious level and is one of the most reliable signals of a person's attraction. Watch out for people mirroring your actions.

There is either a deep-seated need to be accepted or they are truly attracted to you. Sometimes after you've just met or been introduced to a person at a party, you'll notice that he or she starts mirroring everything from your words to your nods to your hand gestures to expressions.

People who don't know much about reading or analyzing people will often miss these clues.

However, on a subconscious level, this is a sign that the person is seeking your acceptance or approval. When you are leaning against the bar, you'll notice a person come up to you and lean in the same position as you before striking up a conversation. They are doing nothing but attempting to mirror your actions in a bid to make you feel that they are one among your kind. People will hold their glass exactly in the manner in which you are holding yours or they may take a sip on their drink right after you do to show you that they are like you. The feeling of affiliating with people on a psychological level drives people to mirror their actions.

Chapter 14 Mirroring

Have you ever sat in a restaurant and people watched? It can be quite amusing to sit back and watch all of the people out and about around you, attempting to identify how their relationships must be going by body language alone. Yes, it is quite possible to understand at the briefest glance at another how they get along. You can absolutely tell how much or how little people get along simply by watching them together and seeing how they naturally orient their bodies around each other. This simple skill is referred to as mirroring, and it is absolutely crucial if you want to be successful at influencing or persuading others. When you understand mirroring, you essentially have a built-in system in which you can judge just how well people are likely to be willing to listen to you. You can tell if you are successful in developing rapport, and if you have not, you will be able to push the act of earning rapport along a little quicker. You can utilize mirroring in a wide range of ways that can absolutely be beneficial to you, and you can utilize it in ways that can be useful to others as well.

What is Mirroring?

First things first, you must learn what mirroring is. At the simplest, it is the human tendency to mirror what is happening around them when they feel a relationship to whatever it is that is around them. For example, if you look at an old married couple, they are likely to constantly be mirroring each other's behaviors. It is essentially the ultimate culmination of empathy—the individuals are so bonded, so aware of each other and their behaviors, that they unconsciously mimic any behaviors that their partner does first. The two married people at the diner may both sip at their coffees at the same time as each other, or if one drinks, the other will follow shortly after. If one shifts in his seat, she will do so as well, always leaning to mirror the position her husband is in. If she brushes off something on her shoulder, he will unconsciously touch his shoulder as well. This act is known as mirroring, and it occurs in a wide range of circumstances.

You do not necessarily have to be a married couple that has been together for decades for mirroring to be relevant, either—you can see it everywhere. The person interviewing you for a job may begin to mirror you when the interview is going well, or the person who thinks that you are attractive may mimic some of your behaviors as well. You can see these behaviors mimicked started quite early on in terms of how long people have been interacting as well—sometimes people will even hit it off right off the bat and begin mirroring each other, emphasizing the fact that they seemed to have clicked.

Mirroring is essentially the ultimate form of flattery—it involves literally copying the other person because you like or love them so much. Children mirror their parents when learning how to behave in the world. Good friends often mirror each other. Salespeople wanting to win rapport, mirror people. No matter what the relationship is, if it is a positive one, there are likely mirroring behaviors, whether unconscious or not.

Uses of Mirroring

You may be wondering why something as simple as mimicry can actually be important to others, but it is actually one of the most fundamental parts of influence, persuasion, and manipulation. When you mirror someone, you can develop rapport. Rapport is essentially the measurement of your relationship with someone—if you have a good rapport with someone, you have developed some level of trust with them. The other person is likely to believe what you are saying if you develop rapport. However, if you have not yet developed rapport yet and you need the other person to listen to you, you can oftentimes artificially create that rapport through one simple task—mirroring. If you mirror the other person, you can essentially convince him to develop a rapport with you, whether it was something he wanted to develop on his own or whether you forced the point.

By constantly mirroring the other person, you essentially send the signs to their brain that they need to like this person because this person is just like them. Remember the three key factors for likability? The first one was able to relate or identify with the other person. In this case, you are presenting yourself as easy to relate to simply because you want the other person to like you. With liking you comes rapport. With rapport comes trust, which you can use to convince the other person to buy cars or do certain things that will benefit you. Building rapport even builds up the ability to be able to manipulate the other person—you need to be trustworthy for the other person to let you close enough to manipulate in the first place.

How to Mirror

Luckily for you, mirroring is quite easy to learn how to do. While it may seem awkward and unnatural at first, the more you practice it, the more natural it will become to you, and the more effective you can get at it. Remember, if you want to mirror someone, you will need to toe the line between too much and not enough. If you are too overt, the other person will catch on and will likely be more put off than convinced to like you. Take a look at these four steps so you can learn to mirror for yourself.

Build up a Connection

The first step when you are attempting to mirror someone is to start by building a connection somehow. If you do not feel the connection with the other person, they are not likely to be feeling a connection either. Keeping that in mind, you should begin to foster some sort of connection and rapport. This can be done with four simple steps on its own.

Fronting: This is the act of facing the other person entirely. You start with your body oriented toward them, directly facing the other person to give them your complete attention.

Eye contact: This is the tricky part—when you are making eye contact, you need to make sure that you get the right amount.

The triple nod: This does two things—it encourages the other person to keep speaking because the other person feels valued and listened to, and it makes the other person feel like you agree with them. It develops what is known as a yes set. The more you say yes, the more likely you are to develop a connection with the other person.

Fake it till you make it: At this point, you have spent a lot of time setting up the connection, and it is time for the moment of truth. You should imagine that the person is the most interesting in the world at that particular moment. You want to really believe that they are interesting to you. Then stop pretending—you should feel that they are actually interesting to you at this point. This is the birth of the connection you had been trying to establish.

Pace and Volume

Now, before you start mimicking their body language, start by paying attention to the other person's vocal cues. You want to make sure you are speaking at the same speed as the other person. If they are a quick speaker, you should also speak quickly, and if they are a slower speaker, you should slow your own speaking pace down to match. From there, make sure you are also mimicking the volume. If they are louder, you should raise your own voice. If they are keeping their voice down, you should follow suit. These vocal cues are far easier to mimic undetected than the rest of the physical cues.

The Punctuator

Everyone has a punctuator they use for emphasis. It could be something like a hand gesture that is used every time they want to emphasize something, or it could be the way they raise their brows as they say the word they want to stress. No matter what the punctuator is, you should identify what it is and seek to mimic it at the moment. Now, oftentimes, this cue is entirely unconscious on the other person's part, and as you begin to mimic it, the other person is likely to believe that you are on the same wavelength. This should really do it for you without making what you are doing obviously.

The Moment of Truth

Now, you are ready to test whether you have successfully built up the rapport you need. When you want to know if the other person has officially been connected to you, you should make some small action that is unrelated to what you are doing at that particular moment and see if the other person does it back. For example, if you are having a conversation about computers, you may reach up and rub your forehead for a split second. Watch and see if the other person also rubs at their forehead right after you. If they do, they have connected to you, and you can begin to move forward with your persuasive techniques.

Chapter 15 Body Language Applications

B ody language and self-esteem go hand in hand. This allows for a wonderful mechanism to observe and monitor how people behave and feel. Awareness of our body language is essential for becoming effective and persuasive communicators. Hence, there are several applications for using, reading, and changing body language.

Therapeutic Applications

Body language plays a major role in counseling, NLP, and hypnotherapy. For psychologists, body language not only allows them a way to read their clients' emotional state, but also gives them a way to build rapport. Observing the client's body language can help the psychologist to read how the client responds to a certain discussion or line of questioning.

Body language speaks when we can't. Health care professionals have known this for some time. A great many studies have been conducted in it, and psychology academic studies for professionals including modalities on body language.

Common issues which can be examined and treated through the use of body language include:

Bi polarity

Individuals with this condition suffer a chemical imbalance that leads to severe depression and the inability to make decisions. They often have a low self-esteem that accompanies this disorder, and it is incredibly difficult to understand effectively or treat correctly. Using body language, the person with bipolarity can be taught to manage their daily situations, and considering the link between body language and emotion, they can also enjoy relief by being trained to use positive body language. This is a way for them to use their own body language to persuade their emotions to stabilize and improve. For their families, body language reading is also an effective way to monitor their loved one's state and intervene before incidents happen. Depression can often go unnoticed and people will rarely speak out about it. They are not likely to say: "I'm feeling depressed."

Low self-esteem

Many of us have suffered the devastating effects of low self-esteem in one way or another. The first victim is our ability to progress in life. A positive belief in yourself is needed if you are to convince the rest of the world to believe in you. People can be trained in positive body language such as the open position, making eye contact, lifting the head. It's a case of faking it until you feel it. With enough repetitive use of persuasive body language, you can even convince yourself that you are stronger than you believe.

Trauma

Survivors of trauma suffer from a loss of power, feelings of inadequacy, and loss of confidence. They also have the burden of guilt where they hold themselves responsible for what happened to them. Whether the trauma is due to a violent act such as an assault or rape, a natural disaster or loss in their family, the emotional state of these individuals is reflected in their body language or the change thereof. Where body language may have been positive and inviting before the incident, the person may now display negative body language, such as crossed arms, slumping, excessive facial touching, and nervous ticks such as repetitive movement. With effective counseling, their progress to recovery can be tracked through counseling and monitoring their body language.

Abuse

Abuse can be physical, emotional, and sexual in nature, but whichever of these it is, there is bound to be an overwhelming sense of a loss of power. The victim may need to be convinced that they can regain their power and that it is okay to trust people. Body language is extremely efficient in this regard. Helping these survivors of abuse establish strong body language will increase their sense of their own strength. Suffering abuse at the hands of another human being is also linked to a loss of trust in people and the world around them.

By helping the abuse victim to understand the body language of others, they can be aided in evaluating the world and those around them in terms of what they see, not what they fear. This is in itself already great empowerment to the abuse victim, as they can become a participant in life again, and feel like they have the power to make informed decisions.

Self-development

Being an effective communicator is one of life's great skills that will open doors and lead to the emboldening of the self. Self-development programs often include modalities on body language where the participants are trained in the uses of positive body language and assertiveness.

Group dynamics

People can be classed as two groups: introverts and extroverts. Introverts, as we know, are those people who tend to thrive in one-on-one communications and prefer to spend more time alone; while extroverts are the life of the party and go through life with a the-more-the-merrier attitude. Introverts often suffer a form of depression based on social settings. They do not do well in groups. As a result, their communication within a group dynamic tends to fizzle. Yet, communication is a learned skill. Like we learn the words, sentence structures, and grammar of a new language, we can also learn the way in which body language works.

Depression

People suffering from depression tend to convince themselves that they are not worthy, that they are to blame for some usually imaginary flaw, and that they are being judged by everyone around them. In the worst cases, this can lead to extreme paranoia.

People with depression sometimes think that everyone else has it good, while they alone are suffering. In creating awareness of body language, they can begin to see the world in a more realistic sense and realize that people everywhere go through trying times and that they are not alone.

By learning to focus on using positive body language they can also begin to manage their condition, as this will encourage feelings of well-being.

OCD

This condition is known for the repetitive behavior that someone engages in to make themselves feel in control of their lives. At the root of this tragic condition lies the fear of a loss of power and a profound distrust in themselves and in others. In extreme cases, this can even extend to excessive washing of hands to remove imaginary germs and then avoiding people because people have germs.

People with OCD tend to have a very negative view of the world, and their only safety comes from their repetitive behaviors. Using body language, they can be trained to notice positive feelings in others and to begin incorporating that into themselves. As they learn to project a positive self-image, they will feel their stress levels diminish, which will lead to a reduction of their anxiety-driven obsessions. When they feel more balanced, they will begin to develop trust in themselves and those around them.

Destructive body imagery (bulimia and obesity)

Poor body image is a tragic and very destructive condition to suffer from. It goes with low self-esteem, lack of trust, feelings of abandonment, and severe depression. Bulimia leads the sufferer to obsessively lose weight, while obesity is a condition where the sufferer wants to fill themselves due to their own emotional disabilities.

Both these conditions are associated with a loss of reality. These people begin to see the world not as it is, but as they believe it to be, and their world view is almost always negative. They eat, or refuse to eat, to hide from the world and themselves.

Body language is a way to find a connection back to the real world. In reading the body language being projected by those around us, we can begin to see that there are loads of people who are just like us. We are not alone. Using positive body language is one of the therapeutic ways to recover a sense of self that is realistic and beneficial.

The biological feedback mechanism of body language

Due to our loss of trust in other humans, we often turn to animals for comfort and assurance. We read into what people do, what they say, how they say it, and how they react to us. A salesman will do this on a second-by-second basis where they monitor the body language of the client and adjust their body language to match.

Techniques such as mirroring, open position, advancing or retreating, and touching can be used to have an effect on the other person, and monitor how persuasive we are being on them. If they have begun to trust us enough, they will begin to do something we want; in which case, we will trust them since they've done something for us. This endless, nonverbal loop is known as a biological feedback mechanism.

Training and exercises

There are numerous academies and colleges that strive to train people in body language detection and application. They mention facts and case-studies, what to do and what not to do; however, not many of them detail exactly how to improve your body language in a step-by-step way. When considering the activities and desired results, we suggest the following steps be followed:

Observe

Look at the world around you. Notice the people in it and how they interact with each other. Identify people in similar situations to those that challenge you. This could be someone applying for a promotion at work, asking a girl on a date, and even haggling for a discount. Each situation will use the same skills but in different ways. It all boils down to body language.

Take notes if you like, or snapshot the interactions to review later. This may seem like stalking behavior to some, but it is called vicarious learning in psychological circles. You learn from the behavior, whether successful or not, of others.

Practice

This will require some bravery, which is perhaps why people do crazy things in foreign lands where no one knows them. Find some friends, or set up a hidden camera if you have to, or go to obedience training with your dog. The goal is to place yourself in a situation where you can practice some of the skills and how they can be used.

If you feel overwhelmed, you can practice at home with a mirror. You might even find some online help with an online counselor who can perhaps observe you over Skype.

Evaluate

Look at the recording you made of yourself, or talk to friends who are helping you. Don't look at your awkwardness; rather, focus on each body language technique, how you applied it, and what the response to it was.

You may even give yourself a score or write down what you need to focus on. Remember to celebrate the successes, no matter how small. Then it's time to repeat step two, practice.

It may seem like an incredibly arduous task to learn body language, but it certainly is worth it. These skills of using space, posture, facial expressions, eye contact, gesture, and touch are vital to leading a fulfilling life that has less conflict and misunderstanding in it.

Chapter 16 Behavior, Deviant Behavior and Psychology

Behavioral psychology is a field of knowledge that explains the nonverbal movements of the body (facial expression, gestures, intonations) of a person and draws conclusions about how sincere, true, confident and open.

Very often we make such an assessment unconsciously when we feel uncomfortable when we are communicating with, or even avoiding, a familiar person. But we actually appreciate his behavioral manifestations, which tell us what he thinks of us, how he relates, despite the fact that his words may be sympathetic or neutral.

There are a number of techniques for determining a person's true intentions, his emotions, and his level of self-esteem. His movements, facial expressions, and other features reveal his inner fears, attitudes, complexes that we perceive unknowingly or consciously if we have some knowledge and experience.

We perceive the process of communication as a general picture, sometimes during a conversation, we do not notice what we are wearing, what it says, but we pay attention to how it does it, what phrases and words it uses, how it sits and what it holds in our hands. Sometimes the little thing gets attention and is remembered for a long time: smell, speech difficulty, accent, reservations, wrong accents, inappropriate giggles, etc.

The scientific discipline that helps to explain and decipher the unconscious nuances in the behavior of people who give their true intentions is the psychology of behavior.

1. What do gestures and facial expressions tell us?

Facial gestures and expressions play a huge role in the conversation. But despite the simplicity of decoding a person's postures and gestures, they can have a completely different meaning.

For example, in the psychology of lies, there are basic signs of deception: one does not look into his eyes, touch the mouth, nose, neck. But the other person can only touch his nose because of itching.

Crossed legs or arms - these gestures in the psychology of human behavior are interpreted as distrust, tightness, isolation, but the interlocutor may just be cold.

Tips for deciphering manners and gestures can often lead to a dead-end or confuse a person. For example, after seeing the interviewee's open position, confident and calm voice, the pleasant honest look, we consider him an honest man and in fact, he has deceptive intentions. Or pickups, how much charm, wit, sincerity, good breeding they have - and that's all they need to establish themselves.

2.   What do speech and intonation tell us?

Speech speed, rhythm, volume, intonation greatly influence communication and can tell a great deal more information about a person, as behavior psychology considers. Science helps to understand a person's emotional state:

•   A calm, sensible, balanced person speaks rhythmically, slowly, with a moderate level of loudness.

•   The impulsive character gives a quick and lively speech.

•   Those who are not confident or closed-minded speak softly, hesitantly.

3. Often words are not as important as intonation.

But it must be understood that if a person is in an unfamiliar environment, he may behave differently than in a familiar environment.

The psychology of behavior will allow you to identify the hidden factors that actually affect a person. But in order to see and understand them, we need to be "grounded" through knowledge and attentive to people.

Deviant Behavior and Psychology

The phenomenon of such behavior is so complex and widespread that, in order to study it, there is a separate science - deviant theory, which emerged at the intersection of criminology, sociology, psychology, and psychiatry.

1. The concept of "deviant" and social behavior in psychology

"Deviation" from Latin - "Deviation" In psychology, deviant behavior from accepted norms in society is called deviant or asocial. It is a sustainable human behavior that causes real harm to people and society. This is harmful to others as well as to the deviant itself.

The psychology of deviant behavior explores such forms of deviation as suicide, crime, prostitution, drug addiction, wandering, fanaticism, alcoholism, vandalism.

Such behavior is related to anger, violence, aggression, destruction, therefore the society has conditionally or lawfully imposed penalties on the offender of social norms; it is isolated, treated, corrected or punished.

2. The identity of the deviant, his psychology, behavior

Science does not study how and where a person has committed a crime; she is interested in common patterns and personality traits.

Causes and sources of asocial behavior:

• Physiological: genetic predisposition to aggression; endocrine diseases; chromosomal abnormalities.

• Public: imperfect legislation; social inequality; promoting anti-social lifestyle in the media; hangs "labels"; negative evaluations they give to local people.

• Psychological causes: internal conflicts between conscience and desires; special character of the character; mental anomalies; dysfunctional family relationships; too conservative, rigorous, cruel upbringing in childhood.

In the nature of deviations, characteristics such as conflict, negativism, dependence, anxiety, aggression, hostility are common. They often cheat and do it with pleasure, they like to transfer responsibility and blame to others.

A person's deviant behavior leads to social maladaptation, i.e. does not adapt to the conditions of society and, as a result, opposes it.

The child's behavior cannot be asocial as children under the age of 5 have not yet developed self-control and the process of adaptation in society has just begun.

The most dangerous period in terms of the possibility of deviation between the ages of 12 and 20 years.

3. How to deal with behavior problems?

Most often people with such behavior go to a psychologist already in detention centers, in children's colonies, in addiction treatment centers. The society deals with the prevention of deviations in hospitals, schools, the media, but the problem is that there is no individual approach and one cannot handle it alone. But he may realize the need to change his lifestyle and seek the help of specialists.

Psychology of Addictive Behavior

In psychology, addiction is called the science of human behavior, attachment to someone or something. It is unacceptable from the point of view of moral or social norms, endangering the health and causing suffering to the person.

Addiction harms society and humans, limits its development and leads to all kinds of mental illness.

More people die from addiction than crime and war together. It manifests itself as an escape from problems in an illusory ideal world. Gradually the person ceases to control his behavior, emotions, and thoughts. Its entire existence is reduced to the object of dependence, which gradually completely destroys it as a human being.

The widespread use of drugs and alcohol among young people has recently become a national disaster. That is why the attention of psychologists, psychiatrists, sociologists, drug addicts, and lawyers is directed at this issue.

Addictive behavior is also called addiction-this is a kind of deviant behavior. That is, the desire to escape from reality by changing your mental consciousness. Behavioral psychology sees this as a destructive attitude towards itself and society.

Addictive behavior includes alcoholism, drug addiction, smoking, increased libido, gambling, computer addiction, abundant food poisoning, and shopping.

Addiction has different weights, from normal to severe.

Why do some people form this strong and attractive attachment that explains the impulsiveness and frustration of attraction? The answers to these questions are most important for society and all individuals.

Psychology of Gestures and Facial Expressions

The psychology of behavior, gestures and facial expressions are the keys to the secrets of the person he wants to hide. As a result of evolution, man has learned to convey thoughts and feelings through words. But with this skill, he has mastered the art of hiding his true intentions and intentions, aspirations. You should be able to "read" your interlocutor in his gestures. Only in this way can one understand what is in his mind and what can be expected from him.

American psychologist Meyerabian Albert believes that when we communicate, we transmit 7% of the information verbally, 38% in intonation and tone of voice, 55% in non-verbal signals.

The basic rule of the psychology of gestures and facial expression is that there is no person in the world who can fully control the body's movements in the process of conversation, even if it wants to deliberately mislead the interlocutor.

A person at the subconscious level responds almost equally to certain situations. Forced facial expressions and gestures of a stranger allow you to hear and see the words hidden behind the screen.

• Protection. In dangerous or uncomfortable situations, when one wants to isolate himself from the other party - people lean back, close with a book, folder or another object, cross their legs, cross their arms over their breasts, clench their fists. Their eyes are closely watched by those who expect the trick. Such behavior is alert and tense and does not require constructive dialogue.

• Openness. The body is inclined towards the interlocutor, open palms, benign smile - these signals indicate a predisposition to communication.

• Interest. Lack of gestures, talking about enthusiasm, a person full of attention, he leans forward and tries not to move so he doesn't miss a word.

• Boredom. Gone is the sight, the rhythmic shaking of his feet, something in his hands, attraction, yawning. In sign language in the psychology of communication, this means that the listener has no interest in the topic of the conversation.

• Skeptical. The man agrees with the interlocutor but makes it clear that he does not trust such gestures as rubbing the neck, scratching his ear, cheek, forehead, smile, stuffing his chin with his palm.

The psychology of human behavior teaches us to understand the wisdom of non-verbal symbolism and the proper understanding of one another.

What Does Male Behavior Tell Us

The strong half of humanity's psychology is always about performing certain actions. Conquer, win, and conquer. Therefore, in their childhood games, there is always a spirit of endurance, character strength, strength competition

All actions are aimed at the final result. Their self-esteem since childhood is based on ability and achievement.

The words and actions of men and women are different. Therefore, when talking to them, you need to pay attention to the overall behavior. If he sits half turned with his legs and an arm crossed during a conversation and does not listen, he will somehow block the information. When he looks into his eyes and sometimes sees his lips, he is passionate about conversation.

When a man straightens his tie, he changes his posture, raises his eyebrows, opens his eyes-he is interested in the woman who is talking.

If he avoids searching, pulling buttons, or other small details of clothing, covering his mouth with his hand and not keeping his shirt collar straight, the interviewee is trying to hide something.

Note that all these non-verbal signals are average. Strong sex psychology is much more complex and depends on the person and his emotional fullness.

Psychology of Women

The psychology of the beautiful half of humanity is based on several circumstances:

• The nature of the warehouse. Most women are optimistic. They are active, they are characterized by changes in mood, and they are able to control the feelings, subordinate circumstances of their desires.

• Education - What parents put in a little girl determines her actions and behavior.

• Experience - If she has been confronted with negativity throughout her life, she stops believing in people and becomes lonely. Her behavior is different from the standard.

The psychology of a woman's behavior is determined by her attitude towards the man. Psychologists believe that women have natural resourcefulness that helps them in their lives. But they focus their ingenuity on relationships with men. For example, they try to look strong and independent, always have hobbies and hobbies, often plan personal time and so on.

Chapter 17 Interpreting and Understanding Personality Type and their Main Characteristics

G iven this reaction, what kind of personality do you think your boss had? Do you think he would have acted differently if he had a different personality? Yes, he probably would have. But why would a difference in personality have made a change in reaction?

An individual's 'personality' is loosely defined as a collection of traits and characteristics that give people their distinctive character. Throughout the years, there have been countless psychologists who have tried to encapsulate the meaning of a personality - from Freud, to Erikson, to Jung, and many others - and all of these experts have contributed greatly to our understanding of the abstract concept.

Knowing an individual's personality is an important part of decoding people because it tells you how they might act or speak. Their personality will show you their tendencies and social patterns, allowing you to generate a more accurate prediction of how a specific encounter might go.

The Myers Briggs Test

Carl Jung was a Swiss psychiatrist and psychoanalyst who dedicated most of his life to understanding the human psyche. Through his research, he was able to publish several books that gave readers his interpretations and understanding of the human personality. Soon, English translations of these books found their way into the hands of Katharine Cook Briggs - an academic and an avid reader and writer.

Prior to finding Jung's books, Briggs had already developed her own theories on personality. She formulated 4 categories of personality types after noticing that her soon-to-be son-in-law had a different set of characteristics compared to members of their family. Upon reading Jung's books however, she discovered that the psychoanalyst had a far more extensive understanding of personality.

This prompted her to further develop her system, which led to the iconic Myers-Briggs Type Indicator - a personality test that she developed with her daughter, Isabel Briggs Myers. This test is now used widely in employment and school evaluations.

Limitations of the Myers-Briggs Type Indicator

While it is widely used and applied in various fields of practice, the Myers-Briggs Type Indicator isn't without its flaws. In fact, throughout the years, countless critics have made comments about the MBTI's reliability, especially because it can give a person different results with each take.

On top of that, the test does not take neuroticism into account. So, individuals with neurotic tendencies might not be detected by the exam. Finally, the test doesn't provide any accurate measures for what it detects, so it's hard to understand exactly what it tries to understand given that the concept of personality is so abstract.

Even then, using the Myers-Briggs for purposes that include decoding a person can be good enough to get a better understanding of what lies underneath the surface. However, as any cautious detective, you need to be aware of the method's limitations to guide your premises and conclusions.

Attitudes

The first letter in every Myers-Briggs personality type refers to either extroversion or introversion so that each of the 16 types will either appear EXXX or IXXX. This first letter designates the individual's attitude, which was described by Myers as the tendency to act either inwardly or outwardly on thoughts and ideas.

Essentially, extroverts are more inclined to execute action. They move and speak to fuel their motivation. Without this physical manifestation of energy, their motivation has a tendency to decline. People who are introverts are more likely to reflect and think. They prefer inward manifestations of their energy and are more motivated with tasks that require rumination and deep thought.

Here are some of the basic differences of introverts and extroverts:

Extroverts	Introverts
Action oriented	Thought oriented
Prefer a wide knowledge base that crosses over to different concepts	Prefer a deep knowledge base that explains specific information in detail
Enjoy frequent interaction	Enjoy meaningful interaction
Draw energy from socialization	Draw energy from being alone

How do you identify an extrovert or introvert in public?

Of course, drawing this information back to Sherlock, the true value of knowing the attitude types is being able to detect them in real life situations. In this case, you might consider someone an extrovert if they seem to enjoy socializing, if they seem energized with physical activity, and if they present a commanding aura that takes control of interactions.

You might call someone an introvert if they prefer isolation, if they enjoy small meaningful gatherings and socialization, or if they seem energized when given the opportunity to explore ideas, thoughts, and concepts away from the company of other people.

During social interactions, it's possible that someone who is an extrovert might be more interested in direct engagement and conversation. They also tend to be far more vocal about their ideas and opinions, making them quite the challenge to debate with. On the other hand, someone who is an introvert might be much more comfortable having you take the reins of a conversation.

Introverts, as a general rule, are far harder to decode because they internalize everything they think and feel. However, because they are more interested in meaningful interaction, tapping into what they find important and relevant can make it possible for you to get them to become more expressive.

Functions

There are two pairs of functions according to Myers - these are the perceiving and the judging functions. The perceiving functions describe how a person interprets information or data, and the judging functions indicate a person's tendencies when it comes to making a decision based on the facts that have been presented.

The perceiving functions are sensation and intuition. As a general rule, people have dominant traits in a specific dichotomy, but it never means that the other is completely disabled. Everyone has these traits to some extent, it's just that one or the other is more prominent and likely to be used.

Sensation pertains to a method of information processing that uses the 5 senses. This is a more empirical method of data interpretation in which a person prefers to rely on details that are perceivable. They prefer to dwell on data that's present, tangible, and real as opposed to information that comes from hunches or guesswork.

Intuition on the other hand, is a method of information processing that dwells more on the unseen. These people use their gut to feel for the right conclusion, even if that means their conclusion won't be based on factual, tangible information. They're often more interested in the possibilities of the future, so they won't limit themselves to choices that are bound by facts.

The judging functions are thinking and feeling. These are decision making functions that are used when a person needs to arrive at a resolve given a set of information.

As the term suggests, people who use their thinking function to make a decision choose to do so from a somewhat detached standpoint. They use logic and reason and prefer to look at the facts before arriving at a thoroughly thought-out decision. However, that decision affects their emotions or the emotions of others around them isn't a top concern in the decision-making process.

On the other hand, people who use their feeling function when making a decision are more inclined to use the emotional context of the situation instead of simply dwelling on the facts. They prefer outcomes that generate harmony, making choices that suit the benefit and preference of the general census.

According to Jung, each person uses a dominant function in combination with an auxiliary function. The psychoanalyst has also suggested that we use a tertiary function to a much lesser extent, with the fourth function taking the role of a 'shadow'. In all cases, the shadow or fourth function is the opposite of the dominant function.

Lifestyle Preferences

In this dichotomy, there are two options - judging and perception. This is an added facet of the Myers-Briggs Type Indicator which wasn't available in Carl Jung's model. The purpose of this dichotomy is to decipher a person's preference in using either their judging or perceiving functions.

People who manifest the judging function as their lifestyle preference are those who navigate the world using their judging function most predominantly. This means that TJ individuals (or thinking/judging) are seen as logical people, while FJ individuals (or feeling/judging) are seen as empathetic.

In the same way, people who tend to prefer the perception navigate the world using one of the two perceiving functions. That said, individuals who are SP (sensation/perceiving) are seen as concrete individuals who use reliable facts. Those who are NP (intuitive/perceiving) are usually considered or labeled abstract thinkers.

The 16 Personality Types

Although Jung had originally come up with 32 personality types, the Myers-Briggs Type Indicator condensed the types into just 16. These personality types use combinations in each dichotomy to come up with a holistic idea of a person's tendencies.

While it doesn't specifically predict a person's reactions, it does tell you the kind of response you can expect. The personality types shed light on the type of interaction a particular person might prefer, given the specifics they fall into under each dichotomy.

ISTJ	ISFJ	INFJ	INTJ
Sincere, analytical, reserved, realistic, hardworking, responsible, and trustworthy	Warm, considerate, gentle, thorough, pragmatic, devoted, caring, helpful, responsible	Idealistic, organized, compassionate, gentle, prefer harmony, enjoy intellectual stimulation	Original, innovative, independent, strategic, logical, reserved, insightful, driven
ISTP	ISFP	INFP	INTP
Action-oriented, enjoy understanding the mechanical functions of things, spontaneous, analytical	Gentle, sensitive, flexible, helpful, realistic, interested in practicality, strive for a personal space that's logical and beautiful	Sensitive, creative, idealistic, caring, puts great value on inner harmony and peace, focuses on dreams and goals	Logical, precise, reserved, flexible, original, enjoy speculation, can come up with creative solutions to problems, imaginative
ESTP	ESFP	ENFP	ENTP
Outgoing,	Playful,	Enthusiastic,	Inventive,

realistic, action-oriented, curious, pragmatic, skilled negotiator	skilled at negotiating, strong common sense, friendly, spontaneous, tactful	creative, spontaneous, optimistic, supportive, enjoys engaging in new projects	enthusiastic, versatile, inquisitive, strategic, enterprising, enjoys new and unfamiliar challenges
ESTJ Efficient, outgoing, analytical, realistic, systematic, dependable	**ESFJ** Friendly, outgoing, reliable, practical, helpful, prefer to please others, enjoys activity and productivity	**ENFJ** Caring, enthusiastic, idealistic, organized, diplomatic, responsible, skilled communicators	**ENTJ** Strategic, logical, efficient, outgoing, ambitious, long range planners, effective at organizing people

Understanding the personality types entails breaking its corresponding acronym down into parts. The first letter always represents the attitude which would either be extroverted or introverted.

The second and third letters are representative of the functions. As a general rule, this letter combination can't be represented by two letters from the same dichotomy. For instance, an individual can't be both sensing and intuitive since they're both perceiving functions. A person can't be both thinking and feeling since they're both judging functions. That said, the only combinations for the second and third letters can be SF, ST, NF, or NT.

Finally, the last letter in the 4-letter acronym represents the lifestyle preference for that specific personality. This can be either perceiving represented by P or judging represented by J.

All that considered, we can now decipher that a person who falls within the ISFJ personality type - the most common among the population - manifests an introvert-sensing-feeling-judging personality type.

Keep in mind that there's far more to each of these personality types than what's stated in this short table. In fact, each type comes with extensive elaborations that discuss the personality in depth, so it might be worth reading up on the different types to familiarize yourself with each one.

Stocking points of information for each type into your mind palace can help give you keys to understanding each person you encounter based on the type that you identify them to be.

Conclusion

Happy you have made it this far and I hope you found all the information stated here useful for day-to-day life. Explanations on body language and how it can help you decipher what people really think or feel situations. More importantly, we covered how you can use this information to communicate better with people.

Understand if things are a little bit confusing even at this stage—it's supposed to be. The fact is that understanding people is a lifetime process so you will find the need to constantly evaluate your baselines as you move forward.

Here's one thing I want you to remember: you only have control over your own values, actions, and reactions. It doesn't matter how badly you want to connect or forge ties with someone—you cannot make people like you if their values are intrinsically different from yourself. Keep in mind that connection is based on similarities and there's no point connecting with someone when nothing is similar between the two of you. Remember: you matter first. Your values are personal to you and you should NOT allow other people to predict your values.

So what do you do now? Here's what I want you to do:

Take a good look at yourself and assess your own values, personality, communication style, goals, and everything else that pertains to you. I want you to deeply get to know yourself first before attempting to know others.

Your next step would be to observe yourself. What are your mannerisms, your behavior, your tendencies when confronted with specific situations? I want you to know exactly what you're doing wrong and what you're doing right.

Next is cultivating a system of thinking, analyzing, and discovering your own values and motivations before pursuing a behavior. Even before you do something, I want you to pause and think about why you're doing it. What's your ultimate goal and what's the motivation behind it? Feel free to use Maslow's Hierarchy of Needs for this to help you further narrow down your own motivations.

Once you've figured out your goals and motivations, I want you to take a good look at the actions you propose to take. Are those actions in line with your goals and motivations? Will they achieve the results you want? What other roads are there for you to take in order to get the same results, but with much less hindrance on your part?

I encourage you to practice these four steps consistently in order to get to know yourself better and deeper through personal analysis. Only after you're comfortable understanding yourself can you feel comfortable in understanding others. One thing I want you to remember though: you don't have to understand yourself 100%! Face it, people are a mystery and sometimes, we can be a mystery to ourselves too. All I encourage you to do is to try as often and as hard as you can to trace your motivations before pursuing any sort of significant action.

So let's say you're comfortable understanding your own motivations at this point…what about other people? First, I discourage you against reading too much into people you don't know or barely know. While thin-slicing is highly effective, you should not use this as a way to figure out everything around you. People-watching can be fun and a good way to hone your skills, but don't take things too seriously.

Start by focusing only on a small group of people. Make decisions based on conscious "reading" efforts, but keep it simple or in situations where getting it wrong wouldn't have negative consequences in your life. Remember, you're testing the waters here and just honing your skills.

Always keep in mind that this book was written to help you CONNECT with people through developed verbal and non-verbal skills. Hence, try not to use your new superpowers for evil and keep connections in mind when trying to decipher people.

Have a pattern when observing people. This means having a fairly good idea of where to start when attempting to understand them. For example, you look at the feet first, then the hands, then face, or any other sequence you may choose. Having this pre-set programming on where to look gives you a story-type reading experience that can help with any conclusions you might have about the situation. The beauty here is that as you practice this technique, it becomes second nature to the point where you don't even have to consciously guide yourself through the process. Your mind instantly goes to these body parts in order to interpret what they mean.

Learn the art of listening and try not to be too self-absorbed. Even as an extrovert, you should be able to recognize the enjoyment of being able to sit back in one corner of the room and just take in the different movements and reactions of people as they interact with each other.

If you find things too difficult, I suggest you watch a movie multiple times and pay attention not just to the words but also to the actions and movements of the actors. Actors are trained in the proper action and reaction in different situations. Their facial expressions and even the slightest movement of the hands can convey so much and can help hone your skills in prediction. It's by far the safest way of approaching body language understanding while enjoying yourself in the process. Make sure to watch movies with very good actors known for their excellent skills in the art. Meryl Streep movies are perhaps one of the best to do this, focusing primarily on the movement of this amazing actress.

The beauty of watching movies is that there's a way for you to confirm what you suspect about a certain situation. You can look at a person's expression in one scene and guess on what they think or feel. In a later scene, these emotions are often expressed out loud or given further focus, therefore allowing you to really figure out if what you initially thought was correct.

When reading people in the real world, observe and keep your conclusions to yourself. Do not go around telling people that you've "read" how a particular coworker acts and make expressive predictions because of it. I want you to keep any conclusions or ideas you have close to your heart and only use them when needed.

Practice, practice, practice! The beauty of reading body language is that you never run out of people to observe or body language to read. There's always an endless supply of them, so feel free to practice as often as you want. Note though that acting on those observations isn't always advisable. Think about it multiple times before actually making a decision.

Yes—you can read people and making connections simply by honing your verbal and non-verbal skills! But it takes time, patience, and drive. It might seem like such a big project at first, but don't let this stop you! Unless you live under a rock, forging connections and communicating with others is an integral part of your life. You will find that by mastering this talent, you too can achieve a kind of success that only few can boast about.

Printed in Great Britain
by Amazon